MAXnotes®

Henry James's

The Portrait of a Lady

Text by
Kevin Kelly
(M.F.A. Columbia University)
Department of Communications
Andover College
Portland, ME

Illustrations by
Richard Fortunato

Research & Education Association

What **MAXnotes**® Will Do for You

This book is intended to help you absorb the essential contents and features of Henry James's *The Portrait of a Lady*, and to help you gain a thorough understanding of the work. The book has been designed to do this more quickly and effectively than any other study guide.

For best results, this **MAXnotes** book should be used as a companion to the actual work, not instead of it. The interaction between the two will greatly benefit you.

To help you in your studies, this book presents the most up-to-date interpretations of every section of the actual work, followed by questions and fully explained answers that will enable you to analyze the material critically. The questions also will help you to test your understanding of the work and will prepare you for discussions and exams.

Meaningful illustrations are included to further enhance your understanding and enjoyment of the literary work. The illustrations are designed to place you into the mood and spirit of the work's settings.

The **MAXnotes** also include summaries, character lists, explanations of plot, and section-by-section analyses. A biography of the author and discussion of the work's historical context will help you put this literary piece into the proper perspective of what is taking place.

The use of this study guide will save you the hours of preparation time that would ordinarily be required to arrive at a complete grasp of this work of literature. You will be well prepared for classroom discussions, homework, and exams. The guidelines that are included for writing papers and reports on various topics will prepare you for any added work which may be assigned.

The **MAXnotes** will take your grades "to the max."

Dr. Max Fogiel
Program Director

iii

Contents

Section One: *Introduction* 1

The Life and Work of Henry James 1

Historical Background 3

Master List of Characters 6

Summary of the Novel 7

Estimated Reading Time 9

> **Each Chapter includes List of Characters, Summary, Analysis, Study Questions and Answers, and Suggested Essay Topics.**

Section Two: *The Portrait of a Lady* 10

Chapters 1-5 10

Chapters 6-10 19

Chapters 11-15 28

Chapters 16-20 35

Chapters 21-25 45

Chapters 26-30 52

Chapters 31-35 59

Chapters 36-40 66

Chapters 41-45 74

Chapters 46-50 80

Chapters 51-55 85

Section Three: *Sample Analytical Paper Topics* 94

Section Four: *Bibliography* 98

Introduction

The Life and Work of Henry James

Henry James, an American author, spent much of his life living in, and writing about, Europe. As a novelist, short-story writer, and critic, James was particularly interested in Europe's history and traditions and the formal manners of its upper class. His tales of independent, yet naive, Americans encountering the cultivated, subtle influences of European society made him famous, although his work was not fully accepted until years after his death. Influenced by European authors such as George Eliot, Honoré de Balzac, Gustave Flaubert, and Ivan Turgenev, James was a prolific writer, publishing 22 novels and over a hundred short stories. In addition, he is the author of a number of plays, autobiographical writings, and noted critical essays.

Born in New York City on April 15, 1843, Henry James traveled extensively with his parents, Henry James, Sr. and Mary Walsh James, and their four other children. Before he reached the age of 20, James had been to Europe several times, living in Switzerland, France, Germany, and England. His broad education, provided mainly by his parents and private tutors, included the study of literature, philosophy, languages, and religion. Henry, Sr., a wealthy, eccentric essayist and philosopher, knew a number of famous authors and thinkers of the day, including Henry David Thoreau and Ralph Waldo Emerson. This created a unique atmosphere, and exposed young Henry to an impressive array of intellectual and artistic ideas as he was growing up.

In 1860, James suffered a debilitating back injury while fighting a fire at the family home in Newport, Rhode Island. The injury would have a profound influence on him for the rest of his life, affecting his limited romantic relationships, and keeping him from fighting in the Civil War. Unable to participate in the war, James continued his education, studying with private tutors until he entered Harvard Law School when he was 19. His time at Harvard was not a success, however—he was unable to adapt to the rigors of formal education, and he left the school after his first year. Now James began to write seriously and he soon published a short story, anonymously, followed by a series of book reviews and other works of short fiction written under his own name. Much of James's early work reflects his interests in the supernatural, the individual's role in society, and the psychological influences that affect human behavior.

James traveled alone to Europe for the first time in 1869, visiting England, Switzerland, and Italy. Three years later he returned to Europe, touring with relatives at first, then remaining to write and travel on his own. He finally returned to the United States in 1874 and a year later published two books, one a collection of travel essays, and the other a book of short stories. In 1876, he wrote his first novel, *Roderick Hudson*. That same year, James decided to move to Europe, settling first in Rome and then Paris before moving to England where he lived until his death in 1916.

In his early work, such as *Daisy Miller* (1879) and *The Portrait of a Lady* (1881), James explored the theme of Americans encountering European culture. It was *Daisy Miller*, his novella about a young American innocent in Europe, that first earned him widespread recognition and would become his most famous work. In other novels, including *The Portrait of a Lady*, James developed similar themes and characters, but *Daisy Miller* would remain his most popular piece of writing, becoming something of a phenomenon both in America and Europe.

Later, in novels such as *The Bostonians* (1886) and *The Princess Casamassima* (1886), James wrote about revolution and political unrest. His short novels, such as *The Aspern Papers* (1888) and *The Turn of the Screw* (1898), brought him further acclaim, and in the early 1900s, he wrote his last novels, *The Wings of the Dove* (1902), *The Ambassadors* (1903), and *The Golden Bowl* (1904), works considered by many to be his masterpieces.

Although a resident of England for many years, James remained a U.S. citizen until 1915 when, as a political protest over America's refusal to go to war with Germany, he became a British citizen. After James died in 1916, his works were largely ignored until the 1930s, when he was rediscovered in England and the United States. Even today, some readers find his work too abstract and difficult to follow, but others appreciate James's ability to reflect deep thought and human emotion.

James is considered to be a major influence on the work of many authors, including James Joyce, Virginia Woolf, and William Faulkner. He has long been admired for his great literary skill, and his ability to create profound and innovative psychological portraits.

Historical Background

In 1843, the year Henry James was born, the population of the United States was growing, the country's territory was rapidly expanding, and Americans were claiming a more prominent position in world affairs. John Tyler was president, having succeeded President Harrison, who died after only a month in office, in 1841. Adventurous American and European settlers were heading into the western regions of the United States in ever-increasing numbers along the Oregon Trail, and reports of their exploits became the stuff of dime novels and exaggerated newspaper accounts, adding to the growing legend of the wild and woolly American West.

In 1845, the country elected James K. Polk the eleventh president of the United States. A year later, the U.S. Congress declared war on Mexico after hostilities erupted over territory along the Rio Grande border. The United States would eventually purchase the territory, which is now southern Arizona, in 1853 as part of the Gadsden Purchase. The term Manifest Destiny, a justification for U.S. territorial expansion, popularized in 1845, was used to defend U.S. policy during the war with Mexico and throughout the latter half of the nineteenth century as the United States acquired more territory, including Alaska in 1867.

As the United States was expanding its territory, Americans were in the midst of an intense political debate over the question of slavery, the wrenching issue that separated North from South, and it became one of the primary causes of the Civil War. In 1820, Congress had acted on the slavery question, making it illegal north of the territory acquired in the Louisiana Purchase. This action became known as the Missouri Compromise. By 1846, the question had erupted again after the Wilmot Proviso, which would have effectively eliminated slavery, was defeated in Congress after being hotly debated by parties on both sides of the issue. Meanwhile, William Lloyd Garrison, a dedicated abolitionist, was fighting for the immediate emancipation of all slaves. In 1850, in response to the growing abolitionist movement, the Fugitive Slave Law was passed, giving southern slave owners the legal right to pursue and capture runaway slaves who had escaped to free states in the North.

Over the next two decades, while James was growing up, living in both Europe and America, expansion into the American frontier would continue, and the slavery question would remain undecided until the end of the war in 1865. During this time, in the United States and around the world, the impact of the Industrial Revolution was profound. For decades, England had benefited economically from technological advances in agricultural and manufacturing equipment. In continental Europe, Belgium and France experienced industrialization during the 1820s and 1830s, and Germany soon followed, all three becoming powerful industrial nations along with other countries that were able to build and take advantage of a rapidly expanding international railway system.

America, too, was an ideal country for industrialization. In addition to vast amounts of natural resources, the United States had an extensive transportation network, and the country's industrial growth began to have a significant effect on the economies of many European nations. When the Civil War erupted in the United States in 1861, the impact was felt around the world, threatening the growing influence of the United States internationally. Britain and France had particular interest in the war's outcome, but other nations were also affected by it. Following the war, however, industrialization grew, and by the early 1900s, the United States would be outproducing even Britain, manufacturing more coal, iron, and cotton.

As the United States continued to expand and develop, Britain, an ancient country distinguished by its rituals, manners, and social traditions, began to enjoy an atmosphere of political tolerance and intellectual freedom. Britain's rule of law was highly esteemed throughout Europe and the country was economically ahead of its neighbors. In the arts, British novelists such as George Eliot, Robert Louis Stevenson, Charles Kingsley, and Samuel Butler were all making substantial contributions to world literature. Writers in the United States, mindful of the work of their British counterparts, developed literary movements of their own. Important to the Jameses' household were Ralph Waldo Emerson and Henry David Thoreau, authors whose transcendentalist and social theories promoted communitarian living, progressive education, feminism, and the abolitionist cause. Transcendentalists believed in individualism and the sacredness of both humans and nature.

Having grown up in this unique and stimulating environment, Henry James began to write seriously as a young man, and his output was enormous. His work would be studied and praised for generations, but when *The Portrait of a Lady*, an early novel, was published, reviews were mixed; critics seemed uncertain how to judge James's particular form of realism, although all agreed that the novel displayed a masterful use of language. W. C. Brownell, writing for the *Atlantic Monthly*, noted James's ability to carry "the method of the essayist into the domain of romance: its light touch, its reliance on suggestiveness, its weakness for indirect statement...." Horace E. Scudder, also from the *Atlantic Monthly*, wrote that "Mr. James is at great pains to illustrate his characters by their attitudes, their movements, their by-play, yet we carry away but a slight impression of their external appearance; these are not bodily shapes, for the most part, but embodied spirits...." A review in *Harper's* reported that the novel "fulfills all the technical conditions that are essential for the production of a perfect portrait in oil, save those that are mechanical or manual, and manifests clearly enough how successfully the pen may compete with the pencil in the sphere of pictorial art." But Margaret Oliphant, reviewer for *Blackwood's*, complained that, although the book is "one of the most remarkable specimens of literary skill" she had yet seen, *The*

Portrait of a Lady was "far too long, infinitely ponderous, and pulled out of all proportion by the elaboration of every detail...."

~~Undaunted~~ by the critics, James published many works over the next several decades. His writing emerged from the rich atmosphere of the times, and his literary innovations captured the attention of critics and the public during an era of great political and social change in both Europe and the United States.

Master List of Characters

Mr. Daniel Touchett—*A wealthy American banker who now resides in England.*

Ralph Touchett—*Mr. Touchett's ailing son.*

Lord Warburton—*A wealthy English aristocrat and close friend of Ralph Touchett.*

Mrs. Lydia Touchett—*Mr. Touchett's wife and Ralph's mother. She has arrived from America with her niece, Isabel Archer.*

Isabel Archer—*A young American woman who is visiting England for the first time. She is Mr. and Mrs. Touchett's niece, and Ralph's cousin.*

Lilian Ludlow—*Isabel's sister who lives with her husband and children in New York City.*

Edmund Ludlow—*A New York lawyer, married to Lilian.*

Edith Archer—*Isabel's other sister. She lives in the American West with her engineer husband.*

Caspar Goodwood—*A young American businessman who is in love with Isabel.*

Henrietta Stackpole—*Isabel's opinionated friend from America.*

Miss Molyneux—*Lord Warburton's sister.*

Mildred Molyneux—*Warburton's youngest sister.*

Vicar of Lockleigh—*Lord Warburton's brother; a burly ex-wrestler who is now a clergyman.*

Bob Bantling—*Ralph's bachelor friend from London.*

Madame Serena Merle—*A friend of the Touchetts who meets Isabel at Gardencourt.*

Edward (Ned) Rosier—*A young American, living in Paris, who had been acquainted with Isabel's family in the United States.*

Mr. and Mrs. Luce—*An American expatriate couple who are living in Paris.*

Gilbert Osmond—*An old friend of Madame Merle's who is living with his daughter in Italy.*

Pansy Osmond—*Gilbert Osmond's young daughter.*

Sister Catherine—*A nun from the convent in Switzerland where Pansy attends school.*

Sister Justine—*Another nun from the Swiss convent.*

Countess Gemini—*Gilbert Osmond's sister.*

Mr. Hilary—*Daniel Touchett's attorney.*

Summary of the Novel

After her father dies, Isabel Archer, a young American woman, is brought to England by her aunt, Mrs. Touchett. At Gardencourt, the Touchett's grand estate outside of London, Isabel meets her elderly uncle, Mr. Touchett; Ralph Touchett, her cousin; and Lord Warburton, an English aristocrat. Isabel, a charming, intelligent woman, is an instant success in her new surroundings. Lord Warburton takes an immediate interest in Isabel and within a few weeks after her arrival at Gardencourt, the Englishman proposes to her. But Isabel declines his offer; at this stage of her life, she prefers to remain independent.

A few weeks later, Isabel's friend, Henrietta Stackpole, a brash American journalist, arrives in England. Isabel learns that Caspar Goodwood, a young businessman from Boston who had been courting Isabel, has also come to Europe. In London, Isabel meets Caspar and he proposes to her. Isabel turns him down, however, for the same reasons she gave Warburton. She is determined to experience life on her own before settling down with any one person. Disappointed, Caspar promises to wait for her for two years.

The next day, Isabel and Ralph return to Gardencourt to be with Mr. Touchett; the old man is quite ill and on his deathbed.

At Gardencourt, Isabel meets Madame Merle, an American who has been living in Europe for many years. While Ralph and Mrs. Touchett tend to Daniel Touchett, Madame Merle and Isabel become close friends. Madame Merle is an accomplished, sophisticated woman with a mysterious background. Although she gets to know Isabel quite well, Madame Merle reveals little about herself. Meanwhile, Ralph, who is ill himself, asks his father to divide his inheritance, giving half to Isabel. Ralph believes his cousin, whom he loves, should have the means to be fully independent.

After Daniel Touchett dies, Isabel becomes a wealthy woman. She travels with her aunt to Italy, where she again meets Madame Merle. In Florence, Madame Merle introduces Isabel to Gilbert Osmond, an American expatriate widower, and Osmond's innocent young daughter, Pansy. Osmond, who has little money of his own, is an arrogant, refined man, proud of his impeccable taste and exquisite art collection. Madame Merle urges Osmond to court Isabel, and soon Isabel falls in love with him. The Touchetts, however, do not trust Osmond; believing he is after Isabel's money, they advise Isabel not to marry him. But Isabel, independent as ever, refuses to listen to them. Osmond, with his superior attitude, looks down on the Touchetts, despite their wealth and social position. However, he also believes he has fallen in love with the young, inexperienced Isabel. Following her initial meetings with Osmond, Isabel leaves Florence to travel around Europe with her aunt for several months. When she returns to Italy, she and Osmond are reunited. Caspar Goodwood rushes back to Europe to confront Isabel, but now she is determined to marry Osmond.

A few years pass, and now Isabel is unhappily married to the cold and dictatorial Osmond. Although Isabel realizes her marriage is a disaster, the Osmonds portray themselves as a happy couple, interested in entertaining and the arts. In truth, Osmond loathes his wife's independent spirit, her many "bad" ideas, and her friends and family. Isabel is particularly concerned about Osmond's meek, obedient daughter. Pansy, a young woman now, is in love with Ned Rosier, a young man Osmond disapproves of and won't allow Pansy to see. To ensure that Isabel doesn't interfere with his daughter, Osmond sends Pansy to live in a convent.

While trying to find a way to help Pansy, Isabel learns that Ralph is dying. Osmond does not want his wife to go to England to see Ralph, but Isabel is determined to leave. Before Isabel departs for England, Osmond's sister, Countess Gemini, reveals a startling fact: Pansy is actually the illegitimate daughter of Osmond and Madame Merle. Madame Merle engineered the marriage between Isabel and Osmond, knowing Isabel's fortune would ensure a comfortable life for Osmond and Pansy.

Devastated by Countess Gemini's revelation, Isabel arrives in England in time to bid farewell to Ralph. On his deathbed, Ralph tells Isabel that, although she has suffered greatly, she still has a chance of finding happiness. After Ralph dies, Caspar Goodwood comes to Gardencourt to beg Isabel to divorce Osmond and to marry him. He loves Isabel and will always take care of her. But Isabel knows that she cannot forsake Pansy; she has promised never to abandon Osmond's daughter. Isabel also feels that it is her obligation as a "lady" to remain married to Osmond. A few days later, she returns to Italy, alone, without informing Caspar.

Estimated Reading Time

The Norton Critical edition of *The Portrait of a Lady* is 473 pages long. Some of the language and dialogue is dated, and the sentences and paragraphs are rather lengthy. The plot is quite involved. Readers might want to allow at least a week to complete the novel, dividing their reading time into several sessions of three hours each, completing four or five chapters per sitting.

SECTION TWO

The Portrait of a Lady

Chapters 1–5

New Characters:

Mr. Daniel Touchett: *a wealthy American banker who now resides in England*

Ralph Touchett: *Mr. Touchett's ailing son*

Lord Warburton: *a wealthy English aristocrat and close friend of Ralph Touchett*

Mrs. Touchett: *Mr. Touchett's wife and Ralph's mother. She has arrived from America with her niece, Isabel Archer*

Isabel Archer: *a young American woman who is visiting England for the first time. She is Mr. and Mrs. Touchett's niece, and Ralph's cousin*

Lilian Ludlow: *Isabel's sister who lives with her husband and children in New York City*

Edmund Ludlow: *a New York lawyer, married to Lilian*

Edith Archer: *Isabel's other sister. She lives in the American West with her engineer husband*

Caspar Goodwood: *a young American businessman who is in love with Isabel*

✝

Summary

The novel begins with a description of Gardencourt, an historic English country estate. Gardencourt is centuries old and was purchased by Daniel Touchett, a "shrewd American banker." Mr. Touchett is retired now and is an elderly man, enjoying his old age living at Gardencourt with his son, Ralph. We first meet Mr. Touchett in the garden where he sits, wrapped in a shawl, listening to Ralph and a friend, Lord Warburton, discuss their mutual problem of being young, bored, and rich. Warburton, handsome and elegant, stands out in sharp contrast to Ralph, who is thin and ungainly.

As the conversation continues, the old man playfully warns Ralph and Warburton that political and social changes are inevitable, and these changes may upset their current lifestyle. He suggests that what Lord Warburton needs is a pretty woman to occupy his time. Warburton replies that he will settle down only when he finds an intelligent and interesting woman to marry. Then old Touchett reveals that his wife is returning from America with her niece, a young woman none of the men have ever met. The old man teases Warburton, warning him not to fall in love with his American niece.

Later that afternoon, Mrs. Touchett and the niece, Isabel Archer, arrive at Gardencourt. Ralph meets the young woman first and he is immediately captivated by his charming cousin. Mrs. Touchett, who has not seen her husband for a year, has retired to her room and will not see anyone until she is rested and refreshed. We learn that Mrs. Touchett had never met her niece before; the old lady had had a falling out with Isabel's father, who was Mrs. Touchett's sister's husband. Consequently, Mrs. Touchett never visited Isabel's home in the United States. Mrs. Touchett's sister died when Isabel was very young, and Isabel was raised by her father and her grandmother. After Isabel's father died last year, Mrs. Touchett decided to visit her family in America.

Mrs. Touchett has not been home for a year, and it is not unusual for her to be away from England for long periods of time. She is not overly fond of her husband, or of the English way of life. She lives abroad, in Italy, for 11 months each year and only returns to England to visit her family for a month before she leaves again.

Her last trip was to America, where she found Isabel living in her grandmother's house in Albany, New York.

Ralph strolls through the gardens with Isabel. Trying to make a joke, Ralph asks her if his mother has "adopted" her, but Isabel insists that no one will adopt her. "I'm very fond of my liberty," she tells him. Isabel quickly reveals herself to be an independent, intelligent young woman. When Ralph introduces Isabel to Lord Warburton, the Englishman takes an immediate interest in Ralph's attractive cousin.

We learn that, as a little girl, Isabel was not forced to go to school. She had attended a nearby elementary school for one day and then decided the strict regimen wasn't for her. She chose instead to spend her time reading books in the "office" room of her grandmother's house. Isabel is described as being very independent and having an insatiable thirst for knowledge. Mrs. Touchett discovered Isabel in the office, reading, when she arrived at the house in Albany. The two women were immediately at odds, but decided they liked each other anyway.

Isabel's two sisters, Lilian and Edith, are both married and no longer live in the Albany house. Edith is the prettiest of the three sisters. She married an officer of the United States Engineers and lives with him out West. Lilian, a plain, unattractive woman, is married to Edmund Ludlow, a New York lawyer. They have two young boys and live in a brownstone in Manhattan. Edmund and Lilian often argue about Isabel because Edmund does not care for Isabel's "originality." Lilian, however, defends her sister; she was pleased when Mrs. Touchett took Isabel with her to Europe to expose her to more of the world.

Isabel's grandmother's house is being sold to pay off Isabel's father's debts. Isabel loved her father despite the fact that he was a spendthrift and a gambler. After her father died, Isabel met Caspar Goodwood, a determined young businessman from Boston. Caspar was quite attracted to Isabel, and he made the long journey from New York City to Albany just to see her. But Isabel was indifferent and really felt nothing for him, so she did little to encourage the romance.

We also learn that, while Isabel was growing up in Albany, Ralph Touchett was living in England and America, attending

school in the United States and visiting England in the summer. His father, Mr. Touchett, worked in England and made a fortune in the banking industry. When it was time for him to go to college, Ralph returned to England to attend Oxford. Ralph, who has always been very devoted to his father, worked briefly for Mr. Touchett after his graduation from Oxford, but he was forced to leave his job after he contracted a serious lung ailment. Ralph does not believe that he will have a very long life.

After Ralph finishes his walk with Isabel, he visits his mother in her room. He asks her what she plans to do with Isabel now that she has brought her to England. Mrs. Touchett says she plans to visit four European countries with Isabel. After their tour, she will choose two of the countries and let Isabel decide in which one she wants to live. Mrs. Touchett believes her niece should be exposed to more of the world. Ralph tells his mother he thinks Isabel is pretty, but he wants to know more about her. Mrs. Touchett describes Isabel as being as frank and determined as she, consequently, they get along very well. Ralph keeps pestering his mother for more information about his cousin, but Mrs. Touchett tells him to find out for himself.

Later, Ralph takes Isabel on a tour of Gardencourt's impressive art gallery. Isabel, always eager to learn something new, is thrilled as Ralph describes a number of beautiful paintings. She is also curious about the ghost that is rumored to be living in her uncle's house. Ralph teases her about it, claiming that people must experience pain and suffering in life before they are able to see spirits. He tells Isabel he doubts she will ever be able to see one. Isabel says she hopes she will be happy in Europe; she certainly does not want to suffer.

Analysis

James introduces several themes in the opening chapters of the novel. The contrast between European and American attitudes and lifestyles is a recurring motif that will be explored throughout the story. Isabel arrives in England, an independent young American, ready to explore the world and all it has to offer. She is eager to learn about and experience European customs and ideas, but she has no intention of sacrificing her independence. This American independence, delivered directly into the heart of a venerable English estate, is an attribute that will define Isabel throughout the course of the novel. In his essay "The New Isabel," Anthony J. Mazzella remarks that in James's "New York Edition" revision of his novel, which he completed in 1908, 28 years after *The Portrait of a Lady* was first published, the most important characteristic of Isabel is her "freedom and vulnerability." Her destiny, therefore, Mazzella notes, "is at once unlimited and fraught with peril."

The Touchetts, after many years of living in England, have more in common with Europeans than with their fellow Americans. The Touchetts have adopted the wealthy lifestyle of European aristocrats. The description of the lush, historic Gardencourt prepares us for the strikingly different world Isabel is about to enter when she arrives in Europe. Her own home has been sold to pay her father's debts, and although Isabel's freedom is of paramount importance to her, the stability and security of Gardencourt is enormously appealing. As we learn about Isabel's background, the difference between the European and American sides of the family becomes quickly apparent. With the death of her father, Isabel was cast out into the world; with few resources other than her own intelligence and self-reliance, she has, at a young age, an opportunity to test herself in the world. But she is immediately scooped up by Mrs. Touchett, who provides a glamorous alternative to the routine, but very modern, existence of Isabel's two sisters.

Although Isabel's arrival disrupts the staid routine of life at Gardencourt, it is a welcome disruption. To the sickly Ralph, and the bored Lord Warburton, Isabel is a breath of fresh air they both find extremely attractive. The handsome, wealthy Warburton, who presumably could marry any woman he wanted, claims that he only enjoys women who are interesting—a quality, we assume, the females of his circle have, until now, been lacking. After meeting the young American, Warburton announces to Ralph: "You wished a while ago to see my idea of an interesting woman. There it is!"

Old Mr. Touchett is also intrigued by his niece and understands the effect she may have on his son and Lord Warburton. His only desire now, at the end of his life, is to insure Ralph's happiness. Mr. Touchett embraces Isabel with the thought that she may help Ralph satisfy his father's final wish. But as Ralph and Isabel tour

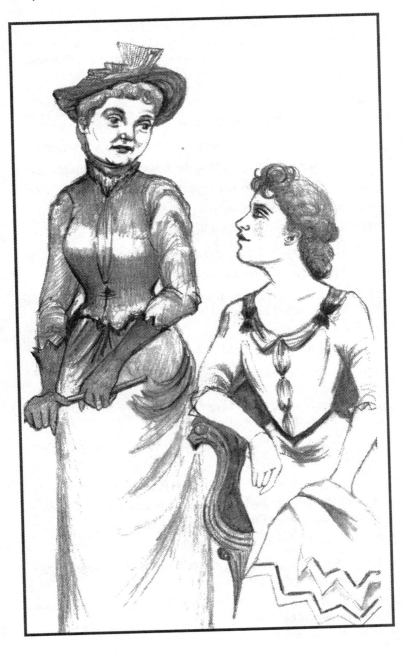

Gardencourt's art gallery, and Isabel wonders about the "ghost" of Gardencourt, James hints that suffering, and not happiness, may one day dominate the lives of both Ralph and his innocent American cousin.

Study Questions

1. What are Ralph and Warburton discussing in the garden?
2. How does Ralph's appearance differ from Warburton's?
3. How does Warburton describe Isabel after he meets her?
4. How did Isabel's father "squander" his fortune?
5. Where does Mrs. Touchett live most of the time?
6. Why did Mrs. Touchett travel to America?
7. How does Edmund Ludlow describe Isabel?
8. What city is Caspar Goodwood from?
9. Where in the United States did Daniel Touchett live before he moved to England?
10. According to Mrs. Touchett, what are American girls "ridiculously mistaken" about?

Answers

1. Ralph and Warburton are discussing their mutual problem of being young, bored, and wealthy.
2. Warburton is a handsome, well-dressed man, while Ralph is homely and ungainly.
3. Warburton calls Isabel an "interesting woman."
4. Mr. Archer spent all his money on gambling and socializing in America and Europe.
5. She lives in a villa in Florence.
6. Mrs. Touchett wanted to look after her investments in America and visit her nieces.
7. Edmund says she is "written in a foreign tongue" and claims he "can't make her out."

8. Caspar is from Boston, although he travels frequently to New York on business.

9. He lived in Rutland, Vermont.

10. Mrs. Touchett says most American girls think they know a great deal about the world, but they are mistaken. In fact, they know very little.

Suggested Essay Topics

1. Why do you think Lord Warburton thinks Isabel Archer is an interesting woman?

2. Why does Mrs. Touchett take such an interest in Isabel? Explain your answer.

3. Discuss the relationship between Ralph Touchett and his father. Why is Ralph so devoted to the old man?

Chapters 6–10

New Characters:

Henrietta Stackpole: *Isabel's opinionated friend from America*

Miss Molyneux: *Lord Warburton's sister*

Mildred Molyneux: *Warburton's youngest sister*

Vicar of Lockleigh: *Lord Warburton's brother; a burly ex-wrestler who is now a clergyman*

Summary

Isabel is described as a young woman with a "high spirit." She is quite determined, has strong opinions, and thinks rather highly of herself. Isabel looks forward to learning as much as she can about the world and hopes she will have the opportunity to prove herself when she is confronted with difficult situations. She is also quick to engage in debate on any subject, with anyone who is willing to take her on. Consequently, most people who meet her find her interesting and appealing.

Isabel's American friend, a journalist, Henrietta Stackpole, is also traveling in Europe. Like Isabel, she is an independent woman, and Isabel greatly admires her. Henrietta has heard that her friend is in England, but since Isabel is traveling with her aunt, it may not be possible for them to spend time together.

Isabel likes to observe herself and is always looking for ways to improve her knowledge and her understanding of her situation. She enjoys living at her uncle's estate and wants to learn everything about England. She spends a considerable amount of time with Daniel Touchett, asking him questions about his adopted country. The old man assures her it is a fine country, filled with good people. Isabel worries, however, that she will be too unconventional for English society, but her uncle assures her that she will be a great success. Isabel quickly forms a close friendship with her uncle.

Because Mrs. Touchett finds England disagreeable, Isabel often argues with her about the country and English customs. She also disagrees with Ralph's opinion of America. Ralph likes to tease Isabel about her patriotism; he has a cynical view of both England and the United States. Ralph, who is often in a melancholy mood, fears his father will die soon and leave him all alone. Ralph would prefer to die first than to be left without his father, whom he greatly admires.

One of the few things that elevates Ralph's mood is the time he spends with Isabel. She is fascinating and attractive, although Ralph dismisses the notion, to himself, that he has fallen in love with her. Ralph understands that his cousin is very independent and is not waiting around for a man to come along and make a life for her. He knows Isabel has her own plans and purpose.

In addition to spending time with her cousin, Isabel also enjoys the company of Lord Warburton. She is curious about English society and wants to meet more people. When Lord Warburton visits again, he stays for a few days, spending a lot of time with Isabel. One night, Mrs. Touchett, Isabel, Ralph, and Warburton stay up, talking in front of the fire. Although Isabel is enjoying herself, when Mrs. Touchett rises to go to her room, she insists that Isabel retire also. She tells her niece that in England it is not proper for a young woman to stay up talking to young men by herself. Ralph and Warburton are annoyed by this, and Isabel is mystified. Isabel thanks her aunt for the advice, however; she wants to learn all she can about English rules and customs, then she will be able to choose for herself which rules she intends to follow.

During the next few days, Isabel spends her time with Warburton, discussing England and America. Warburton has traveled throughout the United States, but he finds that country confusing. He describes his family to Isabel: he has four sisters and two brothers. Both his parents are deceased. One brother he describes as being "wild and pig-headed." An army officer in India, this brother lives a luxurious life, spending great amounts of Warburton's money. Warburton resents the situation and is considering cutting him off.

Later, Ralph tells Isabel that Warburton is "in a muddle" about his life. He is confused and unable to "believe in himself." Daniel Touchett cautions his niece not to fall in love with Lord Warburton, even though she thinks the young man is charming. He describes Warburton as an upper-class radical, always talking about changing society for the good. The old man finds this amusing.

Two of Lord Warburton's sisters, both called Miss Molyneux, invite Isabel to Lockleigh, the Warburton estate. Isabel accepts the invitation and arrives at the estate with Ralph and Mrs. Touchett. Over lunch, they all have a rousing discussion about Warburton's radical beliefs. Although they admire their brother, the Molyneux sisters are uncomfortable with his politics; they don't like the idea of being forced to change their comfortable lifestyle in accordance with Warburton's beliefs. During the discussion, one of Warburton's brothers, a clergyman, arrives. He is a burly ex-wrestler known as the Vicar of Lockleigh. Isabel greatly enjoys visiting Warburton's family.

Later, Warburton walks with Isabel and invites her to come to his house often. He tells Isabel, "You've charmed me, Miss Archer." Isabel, flustered, makes a joke out of Warburton's confession and says she probably won't be able to visit him again. Warburton then promises to visit her, but Isabel remains aloof and experiences a "certain fear" when she considers what Warburton has said to her.

A few weeks later, Isabel receives a letter from her friend, Henrietta, who has arrived in England. Working as a reporter for *The Interviewer*, Henrietta plans to travel in Europe, sending back

her observations of the country to this American magazine. Isabel informs her uncle of her friend's arrival and Daniel Touchett invites Henrietta to stay at Gardencourt.

Isabel and Ralph meet Henrietta at the local train station. After settling in at Gardencourt, Henrietta begins writing an article about the Touchetts and their grand estate. Isabel learns of the article and persuades her friend not to write about the family. She's afraid it would upset her uncle and cousin. Henrietta, however, is determined to learn more about the English aristocracy. She is fascinated by European high society and wants more information about those who live within this privileged circle. She is eager to "get inside" the proper social circles to discover as much as she can about the English elite. Isabel suggests that Henrietta observe Lord Warburton and write about him, instead. Henrietta agrees and begins her observation of Warburton; however, she remains intrigued by Isabel's family. She wonders why Ralph doesn't have an occupation and demands to know if he feels guilty about leaving the United States. She confronts Ralph with her questions and tells him he should get married. Ralph makes light of her suggestion, but Henrietta is put off by his cavalier attitude.

Later, Isabel talks to her cousin about Henrietta. She tells Ralph that her friend disapproves of some of his comments concerning marriage, but Ralph is merely amused by Henrietta's opinions. Isabel remarks that Henrietta reminds her of the "strong, sweet, fresh odour" of the Pacific Ocean, and she admires her friend's convictions. Ralph agrees, concluding that Henrietta has the "smell of the future—it almost knocks one down!"

Analysis

Isabel's independent nature and quick, inquisitive mind is immensely appealing to everyone she meets. Mr. Touchett is happy to spend long hours in conversation with her, as is his son Ralph. Although both men admire Isabel's free spirit, they also have the means and desire to affect her future. While they believe they have Isabel's best interests at heart—Ralph wants Isabel to have the freedom to pursue her own interests—Isabel wants to test herself against the difficulties of life. We will see that the Touchetts' generosity will make Isabel's life more complicated than she ever imagined.

Isabel's friend, Henrietta, reveals the striking contrast between English and American attitudes and customs. Henrietta, the brash, American journalist, is blunt and outspoken. She is utterly baffled by Ralph, a bored American who acts more like an Englishman and does nothing to earn a living. In fact, it appears that Ralph does very little with his life other than attend to his father and Isabel. The wealthy English do, however, spend a great deal of time expressing themselves using a polite, coded language that gradually reveals the true intent of their message. Henrietta, on the other hand, says whatever she pleases, and although the English find her amusing and refreshing, they are nevertheless taken aback by her frank pronouncements. Isabel, too, is quick to express herself on any number of subjects, but, unlike Henrietta, she is interested in learning the customs and habits of English society, not just to observe and report on them, but because she wants to have the option to choose which ones she will follow. Eager to explore and learn more about the world, Isabel is less judgmental than her American friend and more willing to adapt to her new surroundings. In his book, *The Themes of Henry James*, Edwin T. Bowden writes that both Henrietta and Caspar Goodwood are "two ferocious critics of Europe," and Caspar actually "represents all that Isabel has left behind, a life of honesty, of directness, of tangible purpose." Isabel will discover that her open-minded attitude, while giving her the freedom to embrace new ideas, also leaves her without the defenses of her more critical American friends.

For his part, Lord Warburton confesses he finds America a confusing place, and, although he professes radical opinions, he remains firmly rooted in the traditions of the English aristocracy. He enjoys meeting Henrietta, but he is captivated by Isabel, and soon after meeting the young American, he finds an occasion to tell her how he feels. Because Warburton is such an appealing figure, Isabel instantly senses a threat to her freedom—his words "struck her as the prelude to something grave: she had heard the sound before and she recognised it." Isabel's attitude toward Lord Warburton, recalling perhaps her feelings about settling down with Caspar Goodwood, will reveal much about her independent nature and stubborn determination to live a life of her own choosing. While most would consider the rich, handsome, English lord a

FORTUNATO

perfect and flattering match for a young American woman with little money of her own, Isabel is wary of the life he offers. Later, Isabel will make an important decision about Warburton that will haunt them both for years.

Study Questions

1. How did Isabel distinguish herself when she was growing up?

2. What is Isabel's "chief dread" concerning her personal development?

3. According to Ralph, what kind of "specimen" is Lord Warburton?

4. Is Lord Warburton as "easily charmed" as Isabel thinks?

5. According to Ralph, why is Lord Warburton in such a "muddle" about himself?

6. To what person does Daniel Touchett privately compare Isabel?

7. What is the title of Henrietta's article about the Touchetts?

8. Why is Henrietta so determined to learn more about English society?

9. What does Ralph say when Henrietta confronts him about his lack of an occupation?

10. What does Isabel think of the Misses Molyneux?

Answers

1. Isabel's quick mind and active imagination impressed everyone she met when she was growing up in America.

2. She dreads appearing narrow-minded.

3. Ralph tells Isabel that Warburton is a perfect specimen "of an English gentleman."

4. Warburton says that, although he is not easily charmed, he is charmed by Miss Archer.

5. He is greatly concerned about the injustice and inequality in the world and is confused about his own position of wealth and power.

6. He compares her to Mrs. Touchett, when she was younger.

7. The title of the article is "Americans and Tudors—Glimpses of Gardencourt."

8. Henrietta is writing a series of articles about Europe and the English aristocracy for an American magazine; she enjoys commenting sarcastically on European customs and institutions.

9. Ralph says, "I'm the idlest man living."

10. She is charmed by them and finds them a "kind of ideal."

Suggested Essay Topics

1. Why does Lord Warburton think America is such a confusing country?

2. Do you think Lord Warburton is being sincere when he expresses his "radical" beliefs?

3. What does Ralph mean when he says Henrietta has the "smell of the future" about her?

Chapters 11–15

New Character:

Bob Bantling: *Ralph's bachelor friend from London*

Summary

Mrs. Touchett tells Isabel that she does not like Henrietta and describes the American journalist as an "adventuress and a bore." Later, Henrietta argues with Mrs. Touchett about the relative merits of American hotels and American servants; Isabel's aunt finds both lacking when compared to those found in Europe. Henrietta bluntly tells Mrs. Touchett that she thinks her comments are offensive.

Henrietta tells Isabel that she and Caspar Goodwood sailed to England on the same ship. She encourages Isabel to renew her acquaintance with Caspar, but Isabel is unhappy that he has come to England. She dreads the thought of seeing Caspar again. Henrietta remarks that Isabel has changed since coming to England and is now full of "new ideas." A few days later, Isabel receives a letter from Caspar, who is anxious to see her again and asks her for permission to visit.

As Isabel is reading Caspar's letter, Lord Warburton arrives at Gardencourt. She tucks the letter away and strolls through the garden with Warburton, who confesses that he has come just to see her. Since meeting Isabel, only a short time ago, Warburton says, he has been thinking of her constantly. He realizes that, although he has not known Isabel for very long, he has nevertheless fallen in love with her. He asks Isabel to marry him and pleads with her to think it over. He tells her he is willing to wait a long time for an answer if necessary. Isabel agrees to consider the proposal, and Warburton says this gives him hope. But Isabel tells him, "Don't hope too much. I'm not sure I wish to marry anyone." Warburton insists he will wait for her response.

After Warburton leaves, Isabel thinks about his proposal. She realizes she has been offered a "great chance"—an opportunity for wealth and position—but she believes that marriage would restrict her "free exploration of life" and she can't imagine abandoning that. Sitting alone on the garden bench, Isabel wonders about herself, trying to understand why she responded to Warburton the way she did. Is she really such a "cold, hard, priggish" person? Finally, she returns to her uncle's house feeling "really frightened of herself."

The next morning, Isabel tells her uncle about Lord Warburton's proposal of marriage. The old man says he was aware of it — Warburton had written him a letter three days ago, informing him of his intentions. Isabel believes this was the proper thing for Warburton to do, but she doesn't think she wants to marry anyone at the present time. Later, Isabel considers both her suitors—Lord Warburton and Caspar Goodwood. Caspar is a serious young man who dresses in dull, stiff clothing. A successful businessman, he manages his family's cotton mill in Massachusetts. Isabel knows that she is not in love with him, but she realizes she can't put him

off and will have to deal with his determined pursuit. She also decides not to marry Warburton, and she writes him a letter telling him of her decision.

Henrietta is aware of Isabel's opinion of Caspar. She informs Ralph of her concern regarding her friend, telling him she fears that Isabel has changed since coming to England. She says Isabel is not the same "bright American girl she was" and complains that she is "turning away from her old ideas." Henrietta also believes that Caspar would be a good husband for Isabel; she wants Ralph to invite him to Gardencourt. When Ralph expresses some astonishment at Henrietta's request, the reporter wonders aloud if Ralph is in love with Isabel himself—a charge young Touchett quickly denies. He agrees to write to Caspar and invite him to the estate. Caspar writes back immediately, however, declining the invitation. Surprised at Caspar's response, Henrietta feels she must discover the reason why Caspar refused the invitation. She decides to travel to London on the pretense of seeing more of England, and she asks Isabel to go with her. When Isabel accepts Henrietta's offer, Ralph decides to accompany them to the city.

Prior to their departure for London, Lord Warburton and his sister, Miss Molyneux, come to Gardencourt for lunch. Isabel nervously watches Warburton to see how he will react to her, but he displays no emotion and is as friendly as ever, although he avoids speaking to Isabel directly. During lunch, Henrietta tells Warburton that she has no use for lords and aristocracy, their titles are archaic and should be done away with. Lord Warburton, with good humor, agrees with her, and Henrietta is unable to get a rise out of him.

After lunch, Warburton meets Isabel in the art gallery. He asks her to explain her reasons for turning down his proposal. Isabel tells him that marriage, and the comfortable life Warburton represents, would separate her from the "usual chances and dangers" of life. She does not want to miss out on anything life has to offer. Warburton assures her he does not have the power to protect her from the world; she would be able to experience whatever she wanted, even if she married him. Isabel understands, but is not convinced that marriage is for her. The others join Warburton and Isabel in the gallery. Miss Molyneux invites Henrietta and Isabel to Lockleigh, but Isabel says she will be going away in the near future and won't have time for a visit. Warburton asks her if he will ever be able to see her again. Isabel tells him she hopes so, "very much," leaving Warburton uncertain about her meaning.

Later, Mrs. Touchett informs Isabel that she is aware of Warburton's proposal, but she wonders why Isabel did not mention it herself. Then she accuses Isabel of looking "awfully pleased" with herself now that she's turned down an English lord's marriage proposal. She asks her niece if she thinks she will find a better chance, with another man, somewhere else in Europe. Smiling, Isabel replies that her uncle would never ask her such a thing.

A few days later, Isabel, Ralph, and Henrietta travel to London, where Ralph arranges for the two women to stay at a small hotel. Ralph moves into his father's mansion in Winchester Square, which is empty for the summer season. After they settle into their quarters, Ralph takes the women on a tour of London. They spend several days enjoying the sights, although Ralph is disappointed that most of his aristocratic friends are still out of town for the summer. Alone at night, in the big, empty mansion, Ralph thinks of Isabel, believing she is even more attractive now than when he first met her.

One afternoon, Ralph invites Isabel, Henrietta, and his friend, Bob Bantling, to tea at the mansion. Bob is a 40-year-old "amiable bachelor" who chatters pleasantly to the two women. He invites them both to his sister's home in Bedfordshire. He assures them that his sister, Lady Pensil, has an exciting home, always filled with interesting people. Later in the afternoon, Henrietta goes off to meet some American friends for dinner. Bob accompanies her to town in a hansom cab. Left alone, Isabel and Ralph sit in the garden watching the setting sun. Ralph tells Isabel he knows about Warburton's proposal. He asks her why she did not accept, and Isabel tells him she wants to experience more of life before she marries. After a heated, but friendly, discussion, Ralph says he understands: "You've told me the great thing: that the world interests you and that you want to throw yourself into it." Isabel laughs, saying she really isn't as brave as he thinks, but Ralph believes, on the contrary, that Isabel has a great deal of courage. The sun sets and Isabel, after declining a dinner invitation from Ralph, returns to her hotel alone.

Analysis

By turning down Lord Warburton's marriage proposal, Isabel firmly declares her independence. Although she has little money or prospects for the future, she is determined to enjoy her youthful freedom, and she fears a marriage to Warburton would limit her ability to fully experience all that life has to offer. Isabel believes that wealth and privilege, while allowing one a certain freedom, would in truth be confining; the social restrictions inherent in the position of the English aristocrat would ultimately provide her with a narrow experience of life. Isabel is afraid she will be cut off from the world along with the joys and sorrows of everyday life.

Warburton, however, who has always lived the life of a wealthy aristocrat, knows that he is not immune to suffering in spite of his rank and position in society. But Isabel cannot believe him; only through her own experience will she discover that the suffering she, at her young age, almost aspires to is no romantic ideal. Eventually she will come to know true pain and sorrow.

Isabel's feeling toward Caspar Goodwood is similar to her reaction to Warburton's proposal. Although Warburton is presented as a more dashing, appealing figure, Caspar represents the same limited future that Isabel dreads. Isabel would be happy to never see Caspar again, but he has followed her to Europe, and she knows she will have to deal with him when she sees him again. Caspar is the solid, practical American, offering Isabel the same secure life that Warburton offered, but with none of the noble trappings. According to Bowden in his book *The Themes of Henry James*, Caspar "represents all that Isabel has left behind, a life of honesty, of directness, of tangible purpose. He remains an outsider, a foreigner speaking another language in this exotic world of the arts, and has little in common with the Europeanized characters." Henrietta, however, is Caspar's champion; she is another American not overly enchanted with Europe. Proudly patriotic, she views England with a cynical attitude and is quick to lambaste the Europeans, their cities, and their reserved attitudes and odd social customs. She and Caspar provide the counterpoint to the American expatriates and Europeans that Isabel encounters. Afraid that Isabel is being unduly influenced by her new surroundings, and having her head filled with "new ideas," Henrietta would like nothing better than for her friend to marry Caspar Goodwood. Isabel, however, will continue to ignore the goading and advice of her relatives and friends, determined instead to create her own destiny.

Study Questions

1. What is Mrs. Touchett's opinion of American women?
2. When did Caspar last see Isabel?
3. Prior to proposing to her, how many hours has Lord Warburton spent with Isabel?
4. Why does Henrietta want Isabel to see Caspar Goodwood?
5. What is the "big bribe" Isabel refuses?
6. To what Shakespearean character does Ralph compare himself?
7. Besides Gardencourt, does Daniel Touchett, the wealthy American, own other property in Europe?
8. Do Isabel and Henrietta stay with Ralph while visiting London?
9. According to Warburton, who wears the "Silver Cross"?
10. Does Isabel admire her friend Henrietta?

Answers

1. She says they are the "slaves of slaves."
2. Caspar saw Isabel three months ago in Albany.
3. Warburton calculates he has spent 26 hours with her.
4. Henrietta believes Isabel is changing and becoming too Europeanized; she thinks her friend should reconsider her relationship with Caspar, her American suitor.
5. The "big bribe" is what Isabel calls Lord Warburton's marriage proposal.
6. Ralph says, "I'm only Caliban; I'm not Prospero," referring to two characters from *The Tempest*.

7. Daniel Touchett owns Gardencourt, his grand country estate, as well as a mansion in London. Mrs. Touchett owns a villa in Italy.

8. Isabel and Henrietta stay at Pratt's Hotel by themselves; Ralph stays alone at his father's London mansion.

9. The Silver Cross, a badge of rank, is worn by the "eldest daughters of Viscounts."

10. Isabel has great regard for her friend and calls Henrietta a "brilliant woman."

Suggested Essay Topics

1. Why do you think Isabel offers Warburton hope for the future, even though she has turned down his proposal?

2. Compare Isabel's and Henrietta's view of England and Europeans. Why do you think Henrietta's observations are so harsh and critical?

Chapters 16–20

New Characters:

Madame Serena Merle: *a friend of the Touchetts who meets Isabel at Gardencourt*

Edward (Ned) Rosier: *a young American, living in Paris, who had been acquainted with Isabel's family in the United States*

Mr. and Mrs. Luce: *an American expatriate couple who are living in Paris*

Mr. Hilary: *Daniel Touchett's attorney*

Summary

That evening, alone in her hotel, Isabel receives an unexpected visit from Caspar Goodwood. He tells Isabel he's come to see her because Henrietta wrote to him, informing him that Isabel would be alone at the hotel that evening. Isabel is incensed to hear this

and disturbed by Caspar's visit. She has no desire to see him or to confront him about his feelings for her. But Caspar persists in declaring his love for Isabel, and he asks for her hand in marriage. Isabel replies, as she did to Lord Warburton, that she does not wish to marry anyone. She asks Caspar to leave her alone, and to not contact her for at least two years. "If there's one thing in the world I'm fond of," she says, "it's my personal independence."

Caspar agrees to her request, but he says he is willing to wait the two years if Isabel wants to travel and improve herself. Caspar believes, however, that Isabel will get "very sick" of her independence. Isabel is relieved to hear Caspar's promise, but she promises him "nothing" in return, even though he has agreed to wait for her.

After Caspar leaves, Henrietta returns from dinner. Isabel is angry at her for writing to Caspar and inviting him to the hotel. Henrietta says she is just concerned about Isabel's future. Isabel appreciates her friend's concern, but in the future would prefer it if Henrietta would stay out of her affairs.

The following morning, Ralph arrives with the news that his father is quite ill. He must return to Gardencourt immediately and Isabel decides to go with him. Henrietta has been invited to Bob Bantling's sister's house, and, although she is worried about Mr. Touchett, she cannot pass up the opportunity to get acquainted with members of English high society. She tells Ralph and Isabel that she wants to become the "Queen of American Journalism." Later, when she is alone with Ralph, Henrietta tells him about Caspar's visit. "Poor Mr. Goodwood," Ralph says, without much conviction. Henrietta says she plans to urge Caspar not to give up on Isabel.

Ralph and Isabel return to Gardencourt. The house is quiet; the family and servants are very concerned about Mr. Touchett. Isabel is left alone to wander through the great, silent mansion. As she roams through the house, looking for her aunt, she hears music and encounters Madame Serena Merle playing the piano. A grand, 40-year-old woman, Madame Merle greets Isabel and tells her that, even though old Touchett is ill, she couldn't resist playing her music. Isabel assumes the woman is a European, but she soon learns she is a friend of Mrs. Touchett's from America. Madame

Merle has been living in Europe for many years, however. Before Isabel can learn any more about her, the great physician Sir Matthew Hope arrives to treat Mr. Touchett.

Over the next few days, Daniel Touchett's condition continues to deteriorate. Ralph sits with his father, dreading the thought that the old man may die. Daniel tells his son that he has arranged for his future and assures Ralph he will receive a comfortable inheritance. Ralph, however, cares little for money. He is not extravagant and says he needs just enough money to live a modest, comfortable life. His father respects his wishes and has rewritten his will; he will not burden his son with an excess of property or wealth. Daniel, though, would like to see his son get married, and he suggests that Ralph propose to Isabel. Ralph admits he has taken a great interest in his cousin, but he refuses to admit he's in love with her. He tells his father he doesn't think it would be wise for him to marry considering his lung condition and general ill health. Mr. Touchett urges him to marry, anyway; he hopes his son will be able to find some pleasure in his life. Ralph tells his father that he would be happy if Isabel had the means to pursue her many interests. He cares for his cousin and wants to provide for her, and he is also interested in what this intelligent, independent young woman would do with a fortune. As an observer, Ralph is curious to see what effect great wealth would have on Isabel's life. He asks his father to divide his inheritance of £120,000 and give half to Isabel. Daniel argues that if Isabel were given so much money, it would make things too easy for her, but Ralph believes she would handle the money wisely. After a lengthy discussion, Mr. Touchett finally agrees and promises to change his will, giving Isabel half of Ralph's intended inheritance.

During the next few weeks, as Ralph tends to his father, Isabel and Madame Merle become close friends. Madame Merle is an experienced, thoughtful woman who is interested in Isabel and willing to share her knowledge of the world with the eager young American, who greatly admires her new friend. Although Madame Merle is an accomplished person, she has no regular profession. She is a painter and a musician, and in her life she has known more people "than she knew what to do with." She mentions a man named Gilbert Osmond whom she would like Isabel to meet.

Isabel believes that Madame Merle hasn't a single fault. Ralph, however, is not overly fond of the woman, and for her part, Madame Merle disapproves of Ralph's lack of a meaningful occupation and his obsession with his lung disease. She tells Isabel that she and Ralph used to be friends, but his attitude changed and he no longer likes her. Madame Merle wonders if Isabel will grow to dislike her, too. The best part of her life is over, she says. She is alone, with no children, and is no longer beautiful. Isabel is certain, though, that she will always be Madame Merle's friend. They discuss America, and Isabel's plans for the future, and although Isabel reveals much about herself, she never tells Madame Merle about Lord Warburton or Caspar Goodwood.

After a few weeks at Gardencourt, Madame Merle leaves to visit other friends in Europe. Isabel corresponds with Henrietta, who is still in London; Henrietta never received the promised invitation from Lady Pensil to visit Bedfordshire. But Henrietta has been touring London and its environs with Bob Bantling and, on his suggestion, is planning a trip to France.

Daniel Touchett's health continues to fail. One day, Sir Matthew Hope arrives and leaves several hours later, looking very grim. An hour later, Ralph informs Isabel that his father died that afternoon.

A few weeks after Mr. Touchett's death, Madame Merle comes to the Winchester Square house in London to offer condolences to Mrs. Touchett. The old lady acknowledges that her husband was a good man, although she is not overly distraught about his death. She is selling the London mansion and taking Isabel to Paris. She tells Madame Merle that her husband left almost £70,000 to his niece. Madame Merle is flabbergasted by the news and hints that Isabel must have been quite clever in manipulating Mr. Touchett. But Mrs. Touchett defends her niece, saying Isabel knew nothing about the inheritance until after the will was read. Now Isabel is mourning her uncle's death, and she is confused and uncertain about her new financial position.

Ralph leaves for the Riviera, where he hopes the warm climate will improve his health. Isabel travels with her aunt to Paris. Mrs. Touchett wants to teach Isabel how to handle her new fortune. In Paris, Isabel reunites with Henrietta, who is certain that Isabel's

inheritance will cut her off from the real world. She urges her to leave the money to someone she doesn't like since she thinks it will only cause problems for her friend. Later, they visit Mr. and Mrs. Luce, two American expatriate friends of Mrs. Touchett's, who are now both disenchanted with the new French republic. At the Luces' home, Isabel also meets Ned Rosier, a young American who had been acquainted with Isabel's family in the United States. Ned is very enthusiastic about Paris and hasn't much use for the United States, an opinion that angers Henrietta.

Henrietta reveals to Isabel that she traveled to Paris with Bob Bantling, and they spent four weeks together, touring around the city. Henrietta has grown quite fond of Bob; she appreciates his good manners, knowledge, and experience. She tells Isabel they were constant companions until Bob returned to England. Henrietta plans to meet him in Italy when she goes there in the spring.

Analysis

Isabel's rejection of Caspar Goodwood again emphasizes the development of her independent character. As she did with Lord Warburton, Isabel refuses a tempting proposal that would afford her a safe, secure life. And while defending her personal freedom, Isabel also enjoys rebelling against the well-meaning advice of family and friends. Mrs. Touchett expresses her doubts that Isabel will ever find a better husband than Lord Warburton, and Henrietta tries to persuade Isabel to reconsider her feelings toward Caspar Goodwood. Isabel, however, is determined to follow her own path, a course of action she will later come to regret after she meets Gilbert Osmond.

Ralph, who has a different kind of emotional interest in Isabel, is also intrigued by the choices his cousin makes; he respects her independent nature, but he cannot resist influencing her future. When he arranges for Isabel to inherit a fortune, he is altering the course of her life, he believes for the better. The cynical and practical Henrietta warns that the money will mean trouble for her friend, and Isabel, for her part, is at a loss over what to do with her fortune. But Ralph believes he is giving Isabel exactly what she wants, and he is curious to see what a strong-willed young woman will do with her freedom. Ralph also cares deeply for his cousin, and while he doesn't believe she can ever love him in a romantic way, he still wants to do everything he can for her. He has her best interests at heart when he sacrifices half of his inheritance. Later, Ralph will have misgivings about the role he played in shaping Isabel's future.

When Madame Merle enters Isabel's life, Ralph becomes highly suspicious of this glamorous, talented woman. He hints at his feelings to Isabel, who is nevertheless quite taken with her new friend. Madame Merle is an American who has become thoroughly Europeanized during her years living abroad. In many ways she is perfect in everything she does, and Isabel feels she can learn much from this accomplished woman. But Madame Merle is never really the generous person she seems, and Ralph, who has known her for years, understands that she has her own carefully concealed agenda. Isabel can find few faults with her friend, though, and she dismisses Ralph's warning. Madame Merle becomes Isabel's tutor and, like any good teacher, has an enormous influence over her impressionable charge. Oscar Cargill, in *The Novels of Henry James*, believes that Madame Merle is the "lady" Isabel aspires to be, and even after she has become disillusioned with the woman, Isabel must still "measure herself" against Madame Merle "in terms of self-possession and human dignity." Isabel, who is so eager to learn and maintain her independence, finds a perfect role model in Madame Merle; but the young American's desire to improve herself clouds her judgment about the older woman, who may not be the person she presents herself to be.

Study Questions

1. What does Caspar say he would like Isabel to teach him?

2. Why is Isabel afraid of Caspar "watching" her?

3. How does the independent, adventurous Isabel describe her "idea of happiness"?

4. To what professional "title" does Henrietta aspire?

5. Where was Madame Merle born?

6. Who is Mr. Hilary?

7. Before Ralph talks to him about his will, how much money does Daniel Touchett plan to leave Isabel?

8. What is Madame Merle's "great talent"?

9. Does Mr. Luce like the new French government?

10. Where was Ned Rosier raised?

Answers

1. Caspar wishes Isabel could teach him how to live alone. Unfortunately, Caspar can't imagine living without Isabel.

2. She fears his presence will interfere with her "personal independence."

3. Isabel tells Henrietta that her "idea of happiness" is a "swift carriage, of a dark night, rattling with four horses over roads that one can't see."

4. She wants to be the "Queen of American Journalism."

5. Madame Merle was born in Brooklyn, New York.

6. He is Daniel Touchett's attorney.

7. Daniel Touchett was going to leave Isabel £5,000—a comfortable sum to help her get started in life, but not enough to cause her problems.

8. Madame Merle's "great talent" is her "ability to think," a quality that enables her to plot and scheme while involving herself in the lives of others.

9. No. He is a conservative and finds that Paris is "much less attractive than in the days of the Emperor."

10. Ned was born in New York, but he had been raised by his father in Paris.

Suggested Essay Topics

1. Explain why Henrietta has such a negative view of Isabel's inheritance.

2. Discuss Ralph's feelings toward Isabel. He is wary of Madame Merle's interest in his cousin, but does Ralph also have a hidden agenda regarding Isabel?

Chapters 21–25

New Characters:

Gilbert Osmond: *an old friend of Madame Merle's who is living with his daughter in Italy*

Pansy Osmond: *Gilbert Osmond's young daughter*

Sister Catherine: *a nun from the convent in Switzerland where Pansy attends school*

Sister Justine: *another nun from the Swiss convent*

Countess Gemini: *Gilbert Osmond's sister*

Summary

Isabel travels with Mrs. Touchett to San Remo, Italy, to visit Ralph. Isabel is pleased to see Ralph, but she wants to know why his father left her so much money. Without revealing his own involvement, Ralph tells her it was because old Mr. Touchett liked her so much. Isabel is pleased to hear this, but she worries about the effect the money will have on her life. Ralph assures her, however, that she will benefit from it, and by the time she leaves San Remo, Isabel finds she is more comfortable with her new wealth and status. She recalls her rejection of both Lord Warburton and Caspar Goodwood, feeling now a certain measure of pride at her resolve and in the firmness of her decision.

In Chapter 22, we are introduced to Mr. Gilbert Osmond, a widower, and his young daughter Pansy. Pansy, who is 15 years old, has been attending school at a convent in Switzerland. Two nuns have escorted her to Florence to be with her father, who is trying to decide whether to keep Pansy in school. The good-natured nuns, Sister Justine and Mother Catherine, assure Osmond that they are very fond of his daughter and will certainly miss her. Pansy is also quite upset at the thought of leaving the sisters.

Madame Merle arrives; she is close friends with Osmond and Pansy. She is somewhat cool toward the nuns and urges them to leave, even though Pansy doesn't want them to go. Madame Merle advises her not to think of them and then she won't be sad. Madame Merle then suggests that Osmond acquaint himself with Isabel Archer. Osmond, however, is wary of his friend's advice. Madame Merle tells Osmond that Isabel is well off financially, information that sparks Osmond's interest. Madame Merle believes Isabel would be a good match for Osmond. Although he doesn't care much for the Touchetts, especially Ralph, Osmond promises to visit Isabel. Madame Merle then remarks that it is time Pansy left the convent for good.

Madame Merle next visits Isabel at Mrs. Touchett's villa. She advises Isabel to become friends with Mr. Osmond. Isabel has no objections as she has been meeting a great number of interesting people since her arrival in Italy and would enjoy meeting more. Madame Merle also suggests that Isabel become acquainted with a large number of men in order to find out which ones she dislikes. Once she has weeded out the disagreeable ones, she can stay friends with the remaining few. Madame Merle believes Isabel will "despise" most of the men she meets.

Isabel begins touring the museums and galleries of Florence, enjoying the many great works of art on display throughout the city. One afternoon, Madame Merle invites Osmond to tea with Isabel. During the meeting, Isabel is reserved, revealing none of her usual wit and charm. After Osmond leaves, Isabel remains a bit wary of him, although she enjoyed his company. Later, she tells Ralph about Osmond's visit. Ralph is only slightly acquainted with Osmond and does not have any real opinion about him, although he wonders why Madame Merle arranged for Isabel to meet him. Ralph tells Isabel that Madame Merle is a little too perfect in everything she does. He claims to enjoy her company, but he finds her perfection unsettling. When Isabel defends Madame Merle, Ralph decides that the woman would never really do anything to hurt his cousin.

Soon after their first meeting, Isabel again visits Osmond with Madame Merle. At Osmond's home, she meets Pansy and Osmond's sister, the Countess Gemini, who is an elegant, severe-looking woman. Over tea, they discuss living in Italy; Osmond is not overly fond of the place. Afterwards, Isabel takes a stroll with Osmond and he asks her for her opinion of his sister. Isabel demurs, preferring to not offer an opinion based on such a limited knowledge of the woman. As they walk, Osmond tells Isabel that he prefers to live simply, and to lead a quiet life. Isabel does not completely believe Osmond, but she doesn't press the issue. Osmond then says the great joy of his life is his daughter Pansy. Privately, Isabel is impressed with Gilbert Osmond's knowledge and love of art and has decided that she enjoys this man's company and conversation.

Left alone, Madame Merle and Countess Gemini discuss Isabel and Osmond. The Countess believes Madame Merle is manipulating Isabel and has drawn Osmond into the scheme. She is "irritated" with her friend's meddling. But Madame Merle tells Countess Gemini that Isabel has already fallen in love with Osmond, even though she has only met him on two occasions. The Countess thinks Osmond will be a hard man to satisfy; she doubts Isabel would be happy with him. Madame Merle vows not to interfere with either one of them. Then Pansy arrives to serve the two women tea. Countess Gemini asks the girl if she likes Isabel, and if she thinks her father likes her, too. Pansy replies that she thinks Isabel is "charming."

Analysis

In Europe, Isabel is exposed to many of the world's great artistic treasures; she admires the paintings and other art objects she sees, not only at Gardencourt, but also in the many galleries and museums she visits with her family and friends. Isabel's admiration for artists and their work makes her highly susceptible to the charms of Gilbert Osmond. Osmond is first introduced to us as a painter; he is working on a watercolor and has an impressive collection of paintings and other works by various artists. He has excellent taste, and is extremely knowledgeable about the subject of art, while posing as an artist himself. We get the distinct impression, though, that Osmond, who values appearance above all else, is in truth little more than a dilettante with a carefully constructed image. In *The Themes of Henry James*, Bowden describes Osmond's esthetic judgment as "something cold and ugly and evil." Bowden

notes that Osmond's moral judgment is "merely a matter of esthetics," a judgment of "selfishness and egotism, a refusal of the accepted codes of behavior in favor of a private code based on personal taste." Isabel, however, sees none of this when she falls in love with Osmond. Rather, she is captivated by his artistic pretense and sophistication.

Madame Merle is now fully revealed to be a master manipulator. Even Osmond, who can generally hold his own against her, cannot resist her tempting offer of Isabel's fortune. At the same time, both Osmond and Madame Merle struggle for control of Pansy; Osmond's childish 15-year-old daughter obeys every command given by her father and his domineering friend. Pansy, too, is like one of Osmond's pieces of art, and he places her wherever it suits him. Pansy, who hints that she strongly dislikes Madame Merle, would rather stay with the nuns she has grown to love. But Osmond, who is undecided at first about his daughter's future schooling, gives in to pressure from Madame Merle and commands Pansy to stay with him in Italy. Madame Merle seems to have little regard for the girl's feelings when she advises her not to think of the nuns. She merely wants to assert her will, determined that Pansy follow a course she deems best. Madame Merle is satisfied only when Pansy surrenders and learns how to properly serve tea, acting as a little robot without a will of her own. Pansy is devoted to Osmond, but is completely intimidated by him and Madame Merle. She is the opposite of the strong-willed Isabel, whom Osmond plans to reshape, perhaps in his daughter's image.

Isabel's infatuation with Osmond blinds her to the advice Ralph offers about the man. Ralph, always suspicious of Madame Merle, trusts Osmond even less. True to her independent spirit, though, Isabel is determined to keep seeing Osmond. She is more likely to follow Madame Merle's instruction when she is told by her worldly friend, rather ingenuously, to experience a variety of men so that she may learn to weed out the ones she doesn't like. All Madame Merle really wants is for Isabel to marry Osmond. Although at this point in the novel, Madame Merle seems to be nothing more than a clever busybody, later we will learn the real reasons behind her machinations.

Study Questions

1. Why do Isabel and Mrs. Touchett travel to San Remo?
2. What does Pansy think of Madame Merle?
3. What does Osmond say is his "best" fault?
4. Where does Mrs. Touchett live in Florence?
5. Where did Osmond live before he moved to Florence?
6. Does Ralph think Madame Merle is "worldly"?
7. What does Countess Gemini look like?
8. According to Osmond, what is a woman's "natural mission"?
9. What is Osmond's life "plan" that he decided on years ago?
10. What do Madame Merle and the Countess teach Pansy to do?

Answers

1. They go to San Remo to visit Ralph who is staying there, hoping the warmer climate will improve his failing health.

2. Although Pansy never openly expresses an opinion of Osmond's old friend, Madame Merle believes that Pansy doesn't like her.

3. According to Osmond, his "best" fault is his indolence. He apparently enjoys his life of tasteful leisure, even though he is barely able to afford it.

4. Mrs. Touchett lives in an elegant villa known as the Palazzo Crescentini.

5. Osmond originally lived in Rome, and he has been living in Europe for many years.

6. Madame Merle is not just "worldly," according to Ralph, she is "the great round world itself"!

7. She looks like a "tropical bird" with a "long beak-like nose, small, quickly-moving eyes and a mouth and chin that receded extremely."

8. Osmond tells Isabel that a "woman's natural mission is to be where she's most appreciated."

9. "Not to worry—not to strive nor struggle. To resign myself. To be content with little."

10. They teach her the proper way to brew and serve tea.

Suggested Essay Topics

1. Discuss Ralph's role as a confidant to Isabel. If Isabel admires him so much, why does Madame Merle exert the stronger influence?

2. Discuss the relationship between Madame Merle and Countess Gemini. Why do you think the Countess warns Madame Merle not to interfere with Isabel and Osmond?

Chapters 26–30

Summary

Over the next few weeks, Osmond visits Isabel at her aunt's villa five more times. Disturbed by Osmond's interest in her niece, Mrs. Touchett voices her concern to Madame Merle, who claims to know nothing about it. Mrs. Touchett, however, believes Osmond is more interested in her niece's money than he is in Isabel herself. Madame Merle tells Mrs. Touchett she will try to find out if Osmond is honestly expressing his feelings for Isabel. Mrs. Touchett can't understand how Isabel could turn down both an English lord and a wealthy American businessman, yet seem so fascinated by a "middle-aged widower" of limited means. Ralph agrees with his mother, but he doesn't think Osmond is much of a threat; he believes Isabel will have many other suitors before she settles on one to marry. Meanwhile, Isabel continues to see Gilbert Osmond, unaware of her family's concern. She enjoys Osmond's originality, and she loves Pansy, his sweet, "innocent" daughter.

Mrs. Touchett goes on fretting about her niece's interest in Osmond; she does not think highly of the man, or his daughter, and she thinks even less of Countess Gemini. We learn that the

Countess had been married off, by her mother, to an Italian noble-man who is described as a "low-lived brute." The Countess herself is considered to be a shrill, egotistical violator of both "truth and taste." Isabel is willing to tolerate Osmond's sister, despite the woman's unpleasant personality.

In May, Ralph invites Isabel, Bob Bantling, and Henrietta to accompany him on a trip to Rome. All three accept Ralph's invitation, and after Osmond expresses interest in the trip, Isabel invites him to come along. Before he leaves for Rome, Osmond tells Madame Merle he is making progress with Isabel, but he is still unsure about pursuing the relationship. Madame Merle remarks that Osmond is, at times, "quite unfathomable." Why wouldn't he want to marry Isabel? Osmond replies that Isabel is too clever and full of too many "bad" ideas. Osmond believes these notions of Isabel's "must be sacrificed" if they are to have any future together.

The party journeys to Rome, and one day, while touring the city by herself, Isabel happens to meet Lord Warburton. He has been traveling in the Middle East and plans to stop in Rome for several weeks on his way back to England. As he talks to her, it is obvious that Warburton is still in love with Isabel. He confesses that he wrote Isabel several letters but then decided not to mail them. Isabel tells him that she would like to remain friends with him, but only if he abandons his romantic interest in her. Warburton reluctantly agrees.

On Sunday, Isabel's group tours St. Peter's. As Isabel strolls ahead with Osmond, Warburton watches them and asks Ralph about Gilbert Osmond. Ralph tells him that Osmond is an American living in Florence, but other than that he is "nothing at all." Although they would both like to influence Isabel, Ralph and Warburton understand that it is pointless to try to discourage her from becoming involved with Osmond.

One evening, Isabel's group attends the opera. Warburton sits alone in a separate box, keeping an eye on Isabel and Osmond. Osmond notices the special attention the Englishman pays Isabel, and he wants to know more about him. In response, Henrietta makes some sarcastic comments about Warburton's wealth and position. Isabel defends him, though, claiming that he is a "great radical" with "very advanced opinions." From her remarks,

Osmond concludes that Warburton has a romantic interest in Isabel. A few days later, Warburton announces he is returning to England.

After a lengthy stay in Rome, Isabel decides in the spring to return to Florence to join her aunt for a trip to Bellagio. Osmond tells her he fears she will not return for a long time and believes she will probably begin a trip around the world. Isabel wonders if Osmond thinks she is frivolous and accuses him of making fun of her for traveling so much. But Osmond denies the charge; he envies her ability to travel and would enjoy traveling more himself. Osmond then announces that he is "absolutely in love" with Isabel. He realizes, however, that he has little to offer her. Isabel is moved by his words, but she tells him she really doesn't know anything about him. Osmond says he understands and accepts that she is leaving, but he promises that he will eagerly await her return. He decides to stay in Rome for a few more weeks and asks if, before leaving to travel with her aunt, Isabel will visit his daughter in Florence.

Isabel returns to Florence with Ralph and prepares for her trip with Mrs. Touchett. Prior to her departure, Isabel has a disagreement with Madame Merle, who wants to accompany Isabel when she visits Pansy. She doesn't think it will look right if Isabel is seen going to Osmond's house by herself. But Isabel successfully discourages Madame Merle from going with her, and she visits Pansy alone. Pansy is as sweet and charming as ever, chattering away about her father and Mother Catherine. She loves her father, but thinks she loves the nun just as much. She tells Isabel that she is always eager to please her father. Isabel bids farewell to the girl, telling her she will probably not see her again for a long time.

Analysis

Lord Warburton, dignified and refined, appears again to test Isabel's resolve not to marry. At the same time, though, the young American must acknowledge her growing fascination with Gilbert Osmond. The opposite of Warburton in wealth and status, Isabel believes, however, that Osmond possesses an artistic soul and superior intellect. Now that she has her own money, she is truly free to do as she pleases. Warburton's great wealth is no longer a consideration for Isabel; if she wishes to take up with an unsuccessful artist who admits he has little to offer her, she may do so without worrying about her security or future. Both Warburton and Ralph instinctively realize that Osmond is dangerous, but there is nothing they can do to stop Isabel's growing involvement with him. Although Ralph denies that Osmond is a real threat, both men understand that Osmond is completely different from them and this is what makes him appealing to Isabel. In Osmond, Isabel has found someone she believes she can help, a sensitive, intelligent man who will appreciate her own gifts. But far from appreciating Isabel's talents, Osmond is already planning to extinguish Isabel's "bad ideas," the free-thinking independence that men like Warburton and Ralph admire.

Before Isabel leaves on her trip with Mrs. Touchett, Osmond makes her promise to visit his daughter Pansy. Osmond knows he will not be able to see Isabel for some time, but by involving her more intimately in Pansy's life, Isabel will be less likely to forget him and his family. Pansy, innocent and unaware of Osmond's and Madame Merle's scheme, sincerely admires Isabel. When Pansy asks if Isabel will visit her again, Isabel's responsibility to the girl and her commitment to Osmond increases. Osmond proves that he is not above using his own daughter to get what he wants, and he appears to have little regard for Pansy's feelings. In *The Novels of Henry James*, Cargill writes that "Osmond is Henry James's most completely evil character." A man who openly admits he would have liked to have been the Pope because of all the "consideration" the Pope receives, Osmond unabashedly pursues his own shallow interests, and, in the process uses people recklessly and destroys their lives. Isabel, though, remains blind to Osmond's true nature. Cargill notes that Isabel and Osmond are "incompatible from the start, each deceived about the other because neither had any experience with the type of person the other was." Cargill goes on to say that "Gilbert Osmond is wholly evil in his relation to Isabel" and has no moral qualms about his actions.

Study Questions

1. Why is Bob Bantling interested in Henrietta?

2. How does Mrs. Touchett feel about Isabel going to Rome without a chaperone?

3. What is Isabel doing when she encounters Lord Warburton in Rome?

4. What parts of the Middle East did Lord Warburton visit?

5. To what American building does Henrietta compare "Michael Angel's dome" while touring St. Peter's?

6. How does Isabel describe Lord Warburton's "character" to Osmond?

7. What is the title of the sonnet Osmond writes and shows to Isabel?

8. Where does Isabel plan to travel in Italy with her aunt?

9. What are Pansy's greatest talents and skills?

10. What does Pansy like best about Madame Merle?

Answers

1. He thinks Henrietta has a "wonderful head on her shoulders" and he enjoys being with a woman who is not overly concerned with gossip and other people's opinions of her independence.

2. She doesn't approve, but she is resigned to the fact once Isabel decides to go.

3. She is resting, sitting on a "prostrate column near the foundations of the Capitol" by the Roman Forum.

4. He traveled in Turkey, Asia Minor, and Greece.

5. She compares it to the Capitol building in Washington, D.C. and declares the Italian dome suffers by comparison.

6. Isabel says Lord Warburton is "irreproachable."

7. Osmond calls his sonnet "Rome Revisited."

8. Mrs. Touchett plans to take Isabel to Bellagio.

9. Pansy, who is described as "really a blank page," has only "two or three small exquisite instincts: for knowing a friend, for avoiding a mistake, for taking care of an old toy or a new frock."

10. Madame Merle can play the piano and, according to Pansy, "has great facility."

Suggested Essay Topics

1. Discuss Osmond's reaction when he learns that Isabel has refused Lord Warburton's proposal.

2. Other than her desire for a traveling companion, what other reasons might Mrs. Touchett have for inviting Isabel to accompany her on her trip?

3. How do Pansy's feelings for Mother Catherine compare to her attitude toward Madame Merle? Why does Pansy feel so hostile toward Osmond's friend?

Chapters 31–35

Summary

After several months of travel with her aunt, Isabel returns to Florence. Standing by a window in the Touchett home, Isabel recalls the events of the past year: She had been traveling first with Mrs. Touchett, and then her sister Lily, who had come with her family from America to visit Isabel. After saying good-bye to Lily, her children, and husband in London, Isabel traveled to the Middle East with Madame Merle. When she finally returned to Rome, she was reunited with Gilbert Osmond. Osmond stayed in Rome and visited Isabel and Madame Merle frequently for the next three weeks. Isabel then decided to return to Florence to stay with Ralph and Mrs. Touchett. Now, back in Florence, Isabel considers her next course of action.

Shortly after her return to Florence, Isabel receives a visit from a tense and irritated Caspar Goodwood. He is still in love with Isabel and tells her, "I would rather think of you as dead than as married to another man." At this point in the story, we learn that Isabel has decided to marry Gilbert Osmond, but she has not revealed the news to anyone but Caspar and Madame Merle. Upon receiving this announcement from Isabel, Caspar sailed immediately for Italy. Angry and upset that Isabel is marrying Osmond, Caspar was determined to see her one more time. Caspar does not understand Isabel's decision, and Isabel makes no real attempt to defend Osmond or to explain her reasons for marrying him. She says she had thought, once, that she would never marry, but now she has changed her mind. She offers no other explanation and Caspar leaves, furious and hurt. As he walks out the door, Isabel bursts into tears.

After Caspar leaves, Isabel tells Mrs. Touchett about her marriage plans. Mrs. Touchett is very disappointed in her niece. She warns Isabel that Madame Merle manipulated her into the marriage. Isabel finds this hard to believe, even when her aunt tells her that Madame Merle is capable of "anything." Despite her misgivings, Mrs. Touchett accepts the situation and promises to allow Isabel to do as she wishes. Ralph, however, feels "shocked and humiliated" when he hears the news. He has just returned from spending the winter in Corfu, and he is quite ill and looks gaunt and haggard. He blames himself for assuming that Isabel would lose interest in Osmond. Meanwhile, Isabel meets with her fiancé every day, strolling with him through the Cascine, a large park outside Florence.

One morning, Isabel encounters Ralph sitting in the garden of the Touchett estate. Ralph is deep in thought, considering, he tells Isabel, his cousin's impending marriage to Osmond. Ralph admits that he does not approve of the union and doesn't think much of Isabel's intended. Isabel, hurt and insulted, defends Osmond, saying she finds his simple lifestyle admirable. Ralph retorts, "I think he's narrow and selfish. He takes himself so seriously!" Ralph believes Osmond is merely a dilettante, a man not worthy of his cousin. Then Ralph suddenly declares that he loves Isabel, but he has no hope of her ever loving him in the same way.

Isabel is angry that Ralph has such a low opinion of Osmond. Ralph refuses to back down, though, and tells Isabel she is making a great mistake. He berates himself, privately recalling that it was

he who gave his cousin the financial means to allow her to do as she pleases. Ralph says he is sure Isabel will get into serious trouble if she marries Osmond. Isabel bitterly assures Ralph that she will "never complain of my trouble to you!"

Undaunted by her family's opinion of her engagement, Isabel spends long afternoons strolling in the park with Osmond. Osmond is delighted to be marrying Isabel and declares he has never been happier. He knows he is in love with a delightful, intelligent young woman. He thinks they will complement each other perfectly. Osmond also says he is aware that the Touchetts don't approve of him because they believe he is after her wealth. But Osmond assures Isabel that he is not interested in her for her money, and he's certain that he and Isabel will have a wonderful life together.

Pansy is also happy that her father is marrying Isabel. Osmond's daughter is 16 now but still very sweet and innocent. She is looking forward to Isabel joining her family. Osmond's sister, the Countess Gemini, is pleased by the news as well. She tells Isabel she will be a welcome addition to the family. "The Osmonds were once a very good family," she says, but recently they have "dreadfully fallen." The Countess hopes Isabel will be able to help pick them up.

Analysis

Although Isabel spends a considerable amount of time away from Osmond, giving herself time, she thinks, to reflect on Osmond and understand her emotions, she once again comes under the spell of Madame Merle, who is, of course, as eager for Isabel to marry Osmond as the man is himself. During her trip to the Middle East, she spends weeks alone with the conniving, manipulative woman, and when Isabel returns to Rome, she has been primed by Madame Merle to accept Osmond's proposal. It also seems likely that Isabel has been advised to keep the news of the engagement to herself. Isabel has told no one, and she only feels an obligation to inform Caspar Goodwood because he had promised to wait for her for two years. Had Isabel informed her aunt, or Ralph, or Henrietta, she would have received a deluge of negative input regarding her engagement. But, determined as ever to remain independent, Isabel believes she is making her own choice about her future, unaware of the subtle, yet dynamic, influence of Madame Merle.

After she announces her engagement, Isabel does spend time discussing the issue with Ralph, who strongly disapproves of her decision. Refusing to withhold his opinions any longer, Ralph risks alienating Isabel in his attempt to make her see the truth. Ralph dislikes and distrusts Osmond, and he even rashly admits that he loves his cousin, but although Isabel is moved by his sentiment, she cannot be persuaded. With her rejection of an English lord and a successful American businessman, Isabel has proven already that she is quite capable of resisting honest declarations of love. She loves her cousin, but not in a romantic way, and Ralph certainly does not inspire the kind of emotion in Isabel that a Gilbert Osmond does.

Physically weak, and perhaps even homely, Ralph presents a contrast to Osmond in other ways, too. Osmond, the failed artist, whose shallow concerns revolve primarily around his position in society and how he is perceived by members of that society, has a superficial appreciation of the arts. He is more interested in how others view him and in their opinions of his taste and possessions. It is a carefully constructed image and one that Isabel accepts without question. Ralph, on the other hand, has a true artistic sensibility. When he first meets Isabel, he takes a sincere pleasure in showing her Gardencourt's magnificent gallery of paintings. Yet, at the same time, his feelings and concerns for Isabel are genuine, unlike the calculating Osmond. In *The Themes of Henry James*, Bowden asserts that it is this "humanistic attitude" that sets Ralph apart from the other "Europeanized Americans in the novel" and "defines his essentially moral view of life, and increases his bond of natural sympathy with Isabel." Unfortunately, Isabel remains blind to Ralph's sensitivity, humanity, and real concern for her well-being. She spends as much time as she can with Osmond, walking in the park, cut off from her family, and believing herself in love with the man who selfishly seeks to control her as he determines her future.

Study Questions

1. What countries does Isabel visit with Madame Merle?

2. How does Isabel describe Osmond to Caspar?

3. What countries do Isabel and Lily visit together?

4. How does Isabel feel after her confrontation with Caspar?

5. Why is Mrs. Touchett angry at Madame Merle?

6. Why is Ralph "shocked and humiliated" by Isabel's engagement?

7. Why does Ralph think Isabel is in "trouble"?

8. How does Osmond feel about Isabel's inheritance?

9. What does Pansy say when Osmond tells her about his engagement to Isabel?

10. Does Countess Gemini think Isabel will like her husband, the Count?

Answers

1. They spent three months in Greece, Turkey, and Egypt.

2. She says he is a "very honourable man" who isn't rich and is "not known for anything in particular."

3. They meet in France and spend a month in Paris before traveling to Switzerland and then to England, where Isabel sees Lily and her family off as the Ludlows return to America.

4. Although she felt it was her duty to inform Caspar of her marriage plans, she dreaded the thought of seeing him again. After he leaves, Isabel is very upset and bursts into tears.

5. Mrs. Touchett believes that Madame Merle brought Isabel and Osmond together, and manipulated Isabel into accepting Osmond's proposal.

6. Ralph is shocked by Isabel's engagement because he did not take Osmond seriously, and now Isabel, "the person in the world in whom he was most interested was lost."

7. Ralph tells Isabel, in regards to her engagement: "One's in trouble when one's in error."

8. He claims to have no great interest in money, but he doesn't mind having it if it comes his way. "Money's a horrid thing to follow," he says, "but a charming thing to meet."

9. Pansy says, "Oh, then I shall have a beautiful sister!"

10. No. She calls her husband "stupid" and says Isabel "won't care a straw for him."

Suggested Essay Topics

1. Discuss Isabel's feelings for Caspar and Lord Warburton. Why does Isabel "burst into tears" when Caspar stalks out of her aunt's villa?

2. Why do you think Ralph waited so long to reveal his true feelings about Osmond?

3. Do you think Osmond really loves Isabel? Explain your answer.

Chapters 36–40

Summary

A few years have passed. We learn that Isabel has married Osmond and they have recently lost their only child, a baby boy. The Osmonds are living in Rome with Pansy, who has grown into an attractive and charming 19-year-old woman.

Edward (Ned) Rosier, the American we had been introduced to earlier in the novel, has traveled to Rome to ask for Pansy's hand in marriage. Ned met Pansy earlier, in the summer, when they were both staying at a resort in Switzerland. Now, in Rome, Ned approaches Madame Merle and asks her to intervene on his behalf. He believes Pansy loves him and thinks Isabel will not object to the marriage. Ned is wary, however, of Pansy's father; he doubts Osmond will approve. Although she cannot guarantee his success, Madame Merle agrees to help Ned. She warns him, though, that Mr. and Mrs. Osmond are frequently at odds. She advises Ned not to pursue the matter until she has made the proper inquiries for him. Madame Merle then tells Ned how much she admires his

collection of expensive miniatures, hinting that he might want to reward her for her efforts by presenting her with a little gift. After he speaks to Madame Merle, Ned ignores her advice and rushes off to visit Pansy at the Osmonds' villa.

When Ned arrives at their home, the Osmonds are entertaining a number of guests. After he receives a cool reception from Gilbert Osmond, Ned asks Isabel for permission to speak to Pansy, but Isabel tells him that she cannot help him. Ned finally seizes an opportunity to speak to Pansy alone and admits his feelings for the young woman. Pansy declares that she likes Ned, but says little else to encourage him. Meanwhile, Madame Merle arrives and Osmond promptly informs her that Ned Rosier is a bore and is not rich enough to marry his daughter. Madame Merle believes, however, that Ned may be useful to Osmond at some point. She quietly tells Ned to heed her advice and to not approach Pansy again. Then Ned once again appeals to Isabel, who says that she "simply can't" help him.

Ned waits a week before visiting Pansy again. When he does, Osmond bluntly tells Ned that he will not allow Pansy to marry him. Ned seeks out Isabel, but again she refuses to help him, although she hints that Pansy is still interested in him. As Ned is speaking to Isabel, Lord Warburton unexpectedly arrives at the Osmond's home. It has been four years since he last saw Isabel, when he left her with Osmond in Rome. Warburton is an influential politician now. He has traveled to Rome with Ralph, who continues to suffer from his debilitating consumption. Warburton tells Isabel that Mrs. Touchett is visiting America; even though her son is quite ill, the old woman never changes her travel plans.

Isabel is concerned about Ralph's health, but she is happy to see Lord Warburton. The Englishman has apparently gotten over Isabel's rejection of him. Across the room, as Pansy busies herself serving tea to the guests, Ned approaches her. Pansy admits that she loves Rosier, but she will never marry him; her father would never allow it. Crushed, Ned watches helplessly as Isabel introduces Pansy to Lord Warburton, who appears to be quite interested in the young woman.

In Chapter 39, we find out that Ralph and his mother have seen little of Isabel since her marriage to Osmond. The Touchetts still dislike Isabel's husband, and Ralph continues to regret his miscalculation regarding Isabel's intentions toward Osmond. In Ralph's opinion, Osmond is a phony who pretends to be disinterested in society but actually lives to impress everyone he meets. Henrietta has not been in touch with Isabel, either. Her unkind opinion of her friend's new husband matches Osmond's harsh view of Henrietta. Consequently, Isabel's good friend has stayed away from the Osmond household. But Isabel appears, on the surface, to be quite happy.

Following an evening at the Osmond's, Ralph and Lord Warburton discuss their travel plans. Ralph had intended to go to Sicily for his health, but now has decided to stay in Rome. Warburton declares he will stay in Rome also. Both men admit their chief reason for staying there is to be near Isabel. Ralph feels he needs to protect Isabel from Osmond. Warburton agrees, although he is also thinking about Pansy. Ralph is certain Osmond will approve of Warburton's interest in Pansy, considering the Englishman's wealth and status. Ralph wonders, though, if Warburton's real interest isn't in remaining close to Isabel by spending time with her stepdaughter. Warburton protests vehemently, denying Ralph's accusation.

Meanwhile, Madame Merle returns to Rome after spending several months in England and Paris. Isabel is uncertain about her feelings toward Madame Merle; she has not seen much of her friend over the past few years. Osmond claims he has grown tired of Madame Merle and doesn't care if she visits or not. Meanwhile, Isabel and Pansy have become close friends, spending a considerable amount of time together.

One day, Madame Merle visits unexpectedly, and Isabel encounters her having an intimate conversation with Osmond. Later, Madame Merle, who has remained interested in Ned Rosier's pursuit of Pansy, pleads his case to Isabel, who offers little hope for his chances. During this strained conversation, Isabel tells Madame Merle that Lord Warburton is also quite interested in Pansy. Isabel believes Warburton would be a much more suitable husband for Pansy, and Madame Merle quickly agrees. In the future, she says, her "door shall be closed" to Ned Rosier if he asks for her help regarding Osmond's daughter.

Analysis

After years of marriage to Osmond, Isabel appears, on the surface, to be as subservient to him as Pansy. Ned Rosier asks for her help several times, but Isabel continually defers to her husband's wishes. Osmond has now adopted the pose of a wealthy gentleman of leisure. With his new status, he is quick to dismiss Ned, whom he considers unworthy of his daughter, regardless of Pansy's feelings. Although Lord Warburton is considerably older than Pansy, the Englishman's social standing guarantees that Osmond will favor him over a nobody like Ned.

Again, we have the opportunity to observe Osmond, and here he reveals his true nature, completely, for the first time. We quickly surmise that, in the Osmond household, all is not well between husband and wife. Now that Osmond has accomplished his goal of marrying a wealthy woman, he is free to express his narrow, selfish opinions, even if Isabel disapproves of his conduct. Isabel, who has grown even closer to Pansy, has little to say in the affairs of Osmond's daughter, although she cares deeply about what happens to her.

Madame Merle, meanwhile, appears to have lost some of her influence with the Osmonds, although she remains interested in meddling in their affairs. In this case, though, Madame Merle does seem to have Pansy's best interest at heart when she champions Ned Rosier. Ned loves Osmond's daughter, and, while Pansy is hesitant to openly admit it, she loves Rosier, too. But, incredibly, though Pansy is now a young woman of 20, she is still the innocent slave to her father, serving tea and blindly obeying Osmond's every wish. Ned puts his faith in Madame Merle, but the woman soon disappoints him when Isabel tells her of Lord Warburton's interest in Pansy. Madame Merle appears as shallow as Osmond when she declares she will abandon Ned Rosier, preferring Warburton over the young man who really loves Pansy. Isabel also seems to be encouraging the Englishman, claiming to have Osmond's happiness in mind, but perhaps she would like to see Pansy marry Warburton because she herself once rejected him. Now, in her present unhappy state, Isabel may believe that Warburton represents a chance of escape for the hapless Pansy, who is doomed to living life obeying Osmond's whims.

Osmond has succeeded in cutting Isabel off from those who truly care about her. In this way, he is able to maintain control of his wife and their household. Ralph and his mother have seen little of Isabel since her marriage, and Osmond so dislikes Henrietta that he actively encourages his wife to drop the opinionated American as a friend. Osmond continues to chip away at Isabel's resolve in an attempt to banish her "bad ideas." But we sense that Isabel is now fully aware of Osmond's odious character and has no intention of submitting to him, even though it may appear that she is giving in to his demands. Ralph, meanwhile, is aware of his cousin's unhappiness; his predictions about her future have been, regrettably, correct. He arrives in Rome with Warburton, ostensibly to journey south for his health, but with the real intention of providing support for Isabel. Unable to dissuade her from going ahead with a marriage he knew would be "trouble," Ralph is now determined to do what he can to salvage the rest of Isabel's life. Ralph knows he is seriously ill, but he is willing to stay in Rome and sacrifice himself for his cousin. We should remember that Ralph, in addition to loving Isabel, in some ways feels responsible for his cousin's predicament; it was Ralph who arranged for Isabel to inherit her fortune, thus giving her the financial freedom to make all the wrong choices. At the same time, the inheritance made her tempting prey for a fortune hunter like Osmond.

Study Questions

1. Where in Switzerland did Ned meet Pansy?

2. How much money does Ned say he is worth?

3. What is Osmond's opinion of Ned? How does Osmond describe Pansy's suitor?

4. How have the Osmonds established themselves in their wealthy social circle?

5. During their friendly political debates, what name does Ralph call Lord Warburton?

6. If Pansy is not allowed to marry Ned, what does she tell him she will do?

7. Where did the Osmonds move to after their marriage?

8. How has Osmond's attitude toward Madame Merle changed?

9. Why does Isabel think Lord Warburton and Pansy would be a good match for each other?

10. How did Madame Merle learn that Lord Warburton had once proposed to Isabel?

Answers

1. They met at a resort in St. Moritz.

2. He says he has a "comfortable little fortune" of 40,000 francs.

3. Osmond thinks Ned is entirely unsuitable for his daughter. While discussing Ned, he refers to him as a "donkey."

4. The Osmonds attend parties and entertain on a regular basis. Every Thursday evening they host a small party for a select group of friends and acquaintances.

5. Ralph calls him the "King of the Goths."

6. Pansy says she will always obey her father, but if she can't marry Rosier, then she will marry no one.

7. The Osmonds moved to Rome and, with Isabel's money, purchased a villa called the Palazzo Roccanera.

8. Osmond claims he has grown tired of Madame Merle. He says she is "almost unnaturally good."

9. Isabel thinks they are both attractive, but they are also "limited."

10. Mrs. Touchett told Madame Merle about Warburton's proposal.

Suggested Essay Topics

1. Discuss Isabel's relationship with Lord Warburton. How does she feel about the Englishman now that she is married?

2. Why do you think Osmond has gotten sick of Madame Merle?

3. Why do you think Madame Merle is so intent on meddling in Isabel's affairs?

Chapters 41–45

Summary

Isabel believes that Warburton would be a good match for Pansy, and she thinks the marriage would make Osmond happy. Although she is unhappy being married to Osmond, Isabel would like to satisfy herself that she had done all she could to please her husband. When Isabel discusses the matter with Osmond, he agrees that Warburton is the right choice for Pansy. He is annoyed at Isabel, though; it appears to him that she herself still has an interest in Warburton. In any case, Osmond hopes Isabel will use her influence to encourage Warburton to propose to Pansy.

Sitting alone, after her conversation with Osmond, Isabel wonders if Lord Warburton still loves her, and she reflects on how badly her marriage has turned out. Isabel now believes that she and Osmond truly dislike each other. Isabel despises Osmond's pretensions and his desire to live as a fashionable member of society. Osmond, we learn, is angry at Isabel because of her independent mind, her many infuriating "ideas," and her devotion to her cousin Ralph. Isabel understands this and has even tried to change to please her husband, but she will never acquiesce to all of his demands. Resigned to her fate, Isabel has concluded that she will always be unhappy; she has thrown her life away by marrying Gilbert Osmond.

A few days later, Isabel and Pansy attend a grand party together. Osmond stays home, as he usually does, because he doesn't care for parties or dancing. At the party, the two women encounter a lovesick Ned Rosier, who is hoping to dance with Pansy. Pansy, however, has been forbidden by Osmond to dance with Ned, and she spends her time dancing with several other eager young men. As Ned and Isabel watch Pansy dance, Ned again appeals to Isabel to help him. Although Isabel has taken pity on him, she tells Ned there is nothing she can do.

When Lord Warburton arrives at the party, he chooses to sit and chat with Isabel rather than dance with Pansy. Isabel asks him if he really wants to marry her stepdaughter and Warburton assures her that he does, and to prove it, he says he is in the process of writing a letter to Osmond declaring his intentions. On their way

outside, Isabel and Warburton bump into Ned, who is glumly watching Pansy dance. Warburton tells Isabel he feels sorry for the young man and asks how he could help him. Isabel wonders how Warburton could feel that way, considering that Ned is a rival. Warburton, however, doesn't consider him to be much of a threat. Isabel hints that Ned is in love with Pansy, but Warburton does not seem overly concerned. Privately, Isabel tells Ned she will see what she can do to help him with Pansy. Then, as Lord Warburton departs, Isabel reminds the Englishman, somewhat playfully, to send his letter about Pansy to Osmond.

On her way to Rome to visit Isabel, Henrietta stops in Florence and calls on Countess Gemini. The Countess tells Henrietta that Lord Warburton has been spending time with Isabel. She believes that Warburton has renewed his romantic interest in Henrietta's friend. Later, Henrietta meets with Caspar Goodwood, who is also staying in Florence. She hints that Isabel is unhappy and has a troubled marriage. She urges Caspar to go to Rome to see Isabel. Caspar agrees, somewhat reluctantly, but admits he was planning to visit Isabel anyway.

In Rome, Isabel has been visiting Ralph, even though Osmond disapproves. Osmond fears that Ralph will only encourage Isabel's independent ideas. During one of her visits, Isabel and Ralph discuss Pansy and Lord Warburton. They both agree that Osmond would approve if Warburton proposes to Pansy. Ralph believes his old friend would make a fine husband for Osmond's daughter, but he doesn't think Pansy and Warburton are in love with each other. Instead, Ralph hints, Warburton may still be in love with Isabel. Later, when Isabel attempts to find out Pansy's true feelings, Pansy admits she loves Ned Rosier. She also doubts that Warburton really wants to marry her, but she promises she won't marry Ned if her father doesn't approve. Isabel, feeling ashamed of herself for going along with Osmond, advises Pansy to always obey her father. Pansy says she will, but adds that she will probably never marry if she can't have the man she truly loves.

Analysis

Isabel now admits that her marriage is a disaster. She acknowledges that Osmond, the sensitive, intelligent man she was once so taken with, is little more than a shallow egotist. She knows she will never be able to change enough to satisfy him, so they will always be at odds, and Osmond will always hate her. Interestingly, Isabel merely resigns herself to her dismal situation. She never considers leaving Osmond or even confronting him about the sorry state of their marriage. For his part, Osmond remains concerned, as he always has been, with appearances and social standing. According to Bowden in *The Themes of Henry James*, Osmond's moral judgment is "merely a matter of esthetics," and "judgment on the purely esthetic level is the judgment of selfishness and egotism, a refusal of the accepted codes of behavior in favor of a private code based on personal taste. The repellent egotism of such a code is dramatically apparent in Osmond's continual attempt to live only by taste and by appreciation of form, form of the visual and of the social and traditional." Ironically, though, like her husband, Isabel is loathe to reveal any impropriety in her life; in her own way, she cares as much about social convention as Osmond. Her Thursday night gatherings and tasteful home are a source of pride to her even though she despises her husband.

Isabel's modern American friend Henrietta, however, has little regard for appearances or tradition. She has been traveling freely with Bob Bantling, and when she returns to Rome, she understands that she must do something to help Isabel. Still believing that Caspar would make Isabel happy, Henrietta arranges for him to travel to Rome to see her friend. Although she has been unable to see Isabel because of Osmond, Henrietta remains close to her friend; she is not about to abandon Isabel and give in to Osmond's malicious dictates.

Although Isabel can't imagine taking action to end her own marriage, she realizes that at least she can help Pansy. At the dance party, Isabel sees that Warburton is not really interested in Osmond's daughter. Instead of trying to dance with the young woman, Warburton spends the entire evening talking to Isabel; and when he meets Ned Rosier, the Englishman shows only concern for the young man and his morbid feelings. As the dance ends, Isabel tells Ned not to worry about Warburton, saying, "Don't speak of him; I'll do what I can for you. I'm afraid it won't be much, but what I can, I'll do." Isabel has now decided to openly oppose Osmond's wishes.

While Osmond's motives are selfish and mean-spirited, his desire to keep Isabel away from Ralph is understandable; he knows Ralph will only encourage his wife to act against him. Now that Isabel is his wife, Osmond considers her to be another one of his possessions, and like Pansy, he expects to be able to mold her in any way he chooses. Isabel, though, is determined to find a way to make Pansy happy. By discussing the issue with Ralph, she knows that Warburton will learn the truth about Pansy's feelings. She also knows that Warburton is not really in love with Osmond's daughter. At this point, she is no longer concerned about Osmond's happiness, as she was when she was attempting to bring Warburton and Pansy together. A far more important matter is Pansy's future, and Isabel is determined to ensure that Pansy's marriage will be happier than her own.

Study Questions

1. What does Pansy enjoy talking to Lord Warburton about?
2. According to Osmond, what does Pansy have to do to become Lady Warburton?
3. How does Isabel experience the suffering her marriage has brought her?
4. What is Gilbert Osmond's opinion of himself?
5. Does Isabel think that Osmond still loves her?
6. How does Osmond describe Isabel's independent opinions?
7. According to Lord Warburton, why didn't he send his letter to Osmond?
8. How old is Lord Warburton and how old is Pansy?
9. Does Countess Gemini remember who Henrietta is?
10. How does Pansy really feel about Ned Rosier?

Answers

1. "In spite of her simplicity," Pansy is glad to discuss the state of Italy, the condition of the peasantry, taxes, and Roman society with Lord Warburton.

2. Osmond says, "My daughter has only to sit perfectly quiet to become Lady Warburton."

3. Her suffering is described as "an active condition." It was a "passion of thought, of speculation, of response to every pressure."

4. According to Isabel, he thinks he is "better than any one else."

5. No, Isabel now believes that her husband hates her.

6. He says her sentiments are worthy of a radical newspaper or a Unitarian preacher.

7. Warburton tells Isabel that he wasn't satisfied with the letter. He felt it was "awkward" to write.

8. Although Warburton is 42-years-old, he still considers marrying Pansy, who, at 21, is young enough to be his daughter.

9. She doesn't remember Henrietta's name, but recognizes her when she sees her.

10. Pansy tells Isabel that marrying Ned Rosier is the only thing she wanted in life.

Suggested Essay Topics

1. Compare Henrietta Stackpole and Madame Merle. Discuss their motives and the results of their attempts to influence Isabel.

2. Why do you think Isabel changes her mind about helping Ned Rosier?

Chapters 46–50

Summary

   Osmond is concerned about Warburton's true intentions toward his daughter. The Englishman has yet to write the letter he
mentioned to Isabel, and now Osmond is worrying that Warburton
will never keep his promise. Osmond bitterly accuses his wife of
interfering in the matter, a charge she quickly denies. As they are
discussing the matter, Warburton suddenly arrives, finding
Osmond and Isabel in the midst of their heated discussion.
Warburton tells them he has come to say farewell; he must return
to England to attend to an important government matter. It quickly
becomes apparent that Warburton has no intention of proposing
to Pansy. He does invite the Osmonds to England, however, telling
them he thinks Pansy would be a great success there.

   After Warburton departs, Osmond says he thinks Isabel has
been conspiring against him in order to humiliate him. He believes
she is responsible for Warburton's sudden departure. But Isabel
defends herself, claiming that Pansy and Warburton never loved
each other. Privately, Isabel is happy about this turn of events, but
she is saddened to see how different and "strange" Osmond has
become.

   After Warburton has left for England, Henrietta and Caspar
arrive in Rome. Henrietta immediately sees that Isabel is unhappy.
Isabel finally admits to her friend that, yes, she is indeed quite
"wretched." Henrietta wonders why she doesn't just leave her husband, a notion Isabel refuses to consider. Isabel is also concerned
about meeting Caspar again; she is afraid he is still in love with her
and unhappy, but when she sees him, he appears to be in good
spirits and even gets along with Osmond. Meanwhile, Henrietta
begins visiting Ralph, who is now seriously ill and may be dying,
and the two become fast friends.

   Madame Merle, Countess Gemini, and Ned Rosier all arrive
back in Rome at the same time. Madame Merle is immediately
concerned about Lord Warburton and Pansy and wonders why the
Englishman has left Rome.

   In February, Ralph decides to return to England. Henrietta
insists that Ralph "must have a woman's care" on his journey and

announces she will go with him. Caspar has promised Isabel that he will also accompany Ralph back to Gardencourt. Isabel is anxious for everyone to leave; she worries that all her friends are observing her and her unhappy marriage. Isabel tells Ralph she may return to visit him in England, even though Osmond would disapprove.

Caspar visits the Osmonds at one of their regular Thursday night gatherings. He has a pleasant chat with Osmond, telling him he is going back to England with Ralph because he has "nothing else to do." Osmond advises him to marry; if he did, he would find that his time is always occupied. He says he and Isabel have delightful, stimulating conversations and, since getting married, Osmond claims he has never been bored. Caspar, however, doesn't believe Osmond, and when he gets a chance, he speaks to Isabel alone. He says he will go with Ralph to England only because Isabel has asked him to do so. Caspar tells Isabel that he realizes he still loves her, now more than ever. He also knows how unhappy she is in her marriage. But Isabel does not encourage him, and she asks him not to speak of the subject again or he will only spoil his visit.

When Madame Merle learns that Pansy and Warburton are not getting married, she tells Isabel that she is very disappointed. She also reveals that she has been discussing the issue with Osmond, privately. Isabel is crushed when she hears this; she is very hurt that Osmond and Madame Merle would conspire behind her back. Madame Merle asks her if Lord Warburton chose not to marry Pansy to please himself, or to please Isabel. Isabel refuses to answer, angrily asking Madame Merle, "What have you to do with me?" When Madame Merle replies, "Everything," Isabel realizes with horror that her aunt had been right all along: Madame Merle had manipulated her into marrying Gilbert Osmond.

Later, Madame Merle meets privately with Osmond. She feels remorse over her role in bringing Isabel and Osmond together. Her dishonesty and machinations have only brought unhappiness. She warns Osmond not to hurt Isabel, but he dismisses her notions as foolish and leaves abruptly, refusing to listen anymore.

While Osmond meets with Madame Merle, Isabel tours the Roman ruins with Countess Gemini and Pansy. At the Colosseum, they happen to meet Ned Rosier, who tells Isabel that he has sold his precious collection of miniatures for £50,000. Now, he thinks, he has enough money to satisfy Osmond. But Isabel knows her husband will still reject Ned and never allow Pansy to marry him. Osmond will not be satisfied unless Pansy marries an aristocrat. Isabel whisks Pansy away to their carriage before Pansy can speak to Ned herself. Countess Gemini lingers behind to introduce herself to the handsome young man.

A few days later, Pansy tells Isabel that Osmond is sending her back to the convent. He believes she needs to be secluded and enjoy a "retreat" from the world. Isabel knows she will not be able to change Osmond's mind, but Countess Gemini, who has taken up Ned's cause, argues against sending Pansy into exile. Osmond good-naturedly fends her off, but he refuses to change his plans.

Analysis

For the first time, Isabel frankly admits her unhappiness to Henrietta, although she refuses to entertain the notion of leaving Osmond. Isabel hides her feelings, though, from most everyone else, her true expression covered by a "mask," which Edwin Bowden says is an "artificial pose, a false portrait." Later, she is anxious for all her friends to leave Italy; she can't bear the thought of her failed marriage becoming the subject of gossip among them. Osmond, too, insists on maintaining the pretense of a happy marriage. He advises Caspar to settle down, assuring him that his union with Isabel is a source of constant pleasure and satisfaction for him. Later, when Caspar tries to discuss the matter with Isabel, she refuses to admit her true feelings, becoming, in effect, a co-conspirator with her husband, hiding the dismal reality of their marriage from everyone. Osmond's "mask," however, differs from his wife's, says Bowden, in that Osmond's "represents hypocrisy, not generosity, and he attempts disguise to hide his own evil motives." Bowden also notes that as the "full realization of Osmond's aridity and evil comes to Isabel, and she begins to screen the sight of her pain from her friends, she finds herself equally screened in by his pervading egotistic power."

Isabel is now at her lowest point. By admitting her misery to Henrietta, she is also acknowledging it to herself, yet she feels powerless to change her miserable situation. Isabel's shame, and pride, and desire to appear a "lady" have doomed her, at a young age, to a life of regret and sadness. Dorothea Krook, in her essay, "The Portrait of a Lady," notes that it is the discovery of Osmond's "base worldliness and the corrupt values springing from it that first undermines and finally destroys the loving trust in his essential goodness with which Isabel entered into the marriage; and it is this, along with Osmond's egotism, coldness and brutality, that constitutes the betrayal which is the heart of the tragedy."

Ned Rosier is also suffering because of Isabel's husband; he desperately wants to marry Pansy, but Osmond won't let him near her. Ned has even sold his precious art collection, but Osmond's insistence that his daughter marry a man of noble birth makes Ned's sacrifice worthless. Ned will never be the type of man Osmond wants for his daughter, and Pansy won't think of disobeying her father, even though she is in love with Ned. Osmond has molded her into an obedient slave, and it is Pansy's situation that now represents the worst of Osmond's cold-hearted characteristics. Osmond has kept his daughter from feeling any real joy and kept her hidden from the world. When she does, by chance, happen to experience a real emotion and desire of her own, she is not allowed to let it develop. Instead, Osmond plans to shut her away in a convent, where she will be forced to forget, or at least repress, her feelings for the young man who has sacrificed everything for her. Isabel, who is now committed to helping her stepdaughter, is nevertheless unwilling to openly oppose Osmond.

Study Questions

1. Why does Lord Warburton think Ralph should not travel to England with him?

2. How does Lord Warburton feel about Pansy when he decides to return to England?

3. According to Henrietta, what is Isabel too "proud" to do?

4. What is Osmond's opinion of Ralph? Is he concerned about Ralph's illness?

5. Henrietta reminds Osmond of what object?

6. How does Osmond get along with Caspar Goodwood?

7. When does Ralph decide to return to England?

8. If Isabel remains married to Osmond, what does Henrietta think will happen to her?

9. What kind of magazine articles does Henrietta send Caspar Goodwood?

10. What does Osmond say Ned has made him believe in for the first time?

Answers

1. Warburton believes Ralph should wait for warmer weather before he travels, otherwise the cold, combined with the rigors of the journey, could be quite detrimental to his health.

2. Warburton never had any great feelings for Pansy. He is fond of Osmond's daughter and when he leaves, he wishes her happiness for the future.

3. She says Isabel is too proud to admit she made a mistake when she married Osmond.

4. Osmond thinks Ralph is a "conceited ass." He doesn't display any concern over Ralph's deteriorating physical condition.

5. Osmond says Henrietta reminds him of a "new steel pen—the most odious thing in nature."

6. Osmond seems to like Caspar, who, surprisingly, visits the Osmonds regularly at their Thursday night gatherings.

7. He decides to leave Italy toward the end of February.

8. Henrietta worries that her friend's character will become "spoiled."

9. She sends him humorous extracts from American journals.

10. Although he won't allow the young man near Pansy, Osmond says Ned "made me believe in true love; I never did before!"

Suggested Essay Topics

1. Compare Ned Rosier and Caspar Goodwood. Although they are in love with different women, what common bond do they share?

2. Now that Isabel has married Osmond, why does Madame Merle regret meddling in their lives?

3. How does Madame Merle really feel about Osmond?

Chapters 51–55

Summary

Isabel receives word from her aunt that Ralph is gravely ill. If she wishes to see her cousin before he dies, Mrs. Touchett writes, Isabel should come to England immediately. Isabel quickly makes plans to leave Rome, although Osmond disapproves of the trip and would prefer it if Isabel remained in Rome. Ralph, he says, means nothing to him, and he even doubts that Ralph is really dying. Isabel considers Osmond's attitude loathsome; all Osmond is concerned about is keeping up the appearance of a happy marriage. He cares nothing for Isabel's feelings.

Terribly upset by Osmond's remarks, Isabel discusses the matter with Countess Gemini. The Countess is not surprised by the conflict. She knows that relations between Isabel and Osmond are severely strained, and she knows how vicious her brother can be. Countess Gemini then reveals a startling secret: Pansy's mother was not, as everyone believes, Osmond's deceased first wife. Pansy is really the illegitimate daughter of Osmond and Madame Merle. The two friends had actually been lovers for several years when Madame Merle became pregnant with Pansy. Osmond concocted the story that his first wife died giving birth to Pansy. At the time, Madame Merle had also been married. In order to avoid a scandal, Madame Merle never revealed that she was Pansy's mother, but she took an intense interest in the welfare of Osmond and their daughter. She believed Isabel would make a suitable stepmother for Pansy and would be able to provide enough money to allow Osmond and his daughter to live comfortably. Countess Gemini explains that this is why Madame Merle was so upset when Lord Warburton did not propose to Pansy.

Isabel, although stunned by this revelation, finds it in her heart to feel pity for the manipulative Madame Merle. Nevertheless, Countess Gemini urges her to go ahead with her plans to return to England.

Before leaving Rome, Isabel visits Pansy at the convent. Although the nuns are all gentle and friendly, the place still reminds Isabel of a prison. After she arrives at the convent, Isabel is surprised to find Madame Merle already visiting Pansy. Isabel is cool and reserved toward the woman and says little. When Isabel goes up to Pansy's room, she senses immediately that her stepdaughter is miserable. But, obedient as ever, Pansy is willing to stay as long as her father wishes. Isabel asks Pansy if she would like to come to England with her, but Pansy cannot disobey Osmond. But she does admit her dislike for Madame Merle. Without revealing that Madame Merle is her mother, Isabel gently tells Pansy never to say that or even think it again. Isabel promises Pansy she will return for another visit.

After she says good-bye to Pansy, Isabel encounters Madame Merle again in the waiting area of the convent. It is now obvious to both women that their relationship is at an end. Madame Merle spitefully informs Isabel that it was Ralph, and not Daniel Touchett, who arranged for Isabel to inherit her fortune. Isabel is shaken by the news. She tells Madame Merle that she never wants to see her again and is grateful to learn that the woman plans to move to America.

Isabel arrives in England and is met at the train station by Henrietta and Bob Bantling. Before going to Gardencourt, Isabel stops in London and spends the night at Henrietta's flat, where she learns that her friend is planning to marry Mr. Bantling. Isabel is happy for them, although she finds it "odd" that Henrietta is giving up America to live in England after the wedding. Bob is taking the whole thing in stride with his usual good nature. Then Isabel tells Henrietta that she is uncertain about her own future. She admits to her friend that her relationship with Osmond has been "hellish." Henrietta urges her to leave her husband.

In the morning, Isabel travels to Gardencourt to see Ralph. The house is very quiet, and the servants are unfamiliar. Mrs. Touchett, who is sitting with her son, doesn't come down to greet Isabel. Left alone, Isabel wanders around the great house by herself, recalling the last time she was there, when her uncle was dying. Mrs. Touchett eventually comes downstairs to greet her niece. She tells Isabel that Lord Warburton is getting married to an aristocratic English woman. Isabel is surprised, but she refuses to reveal any other emotion upon hearing the news. Mrs. Touchett is still disappointed that Isabel has married Gilbert Osmond. Isabel admits she and her husband don't get along. She also tells her aunt that she has broken off her relationship with Madame Merle.

When Isabel finally visits Ralph, she finds him barely conscious and unable to move. Ralph senses, however, that Isabel is unhappy and he blames himself for it. In a weak voice, he assures his cousin that he arranged for her to inherit her fortune because he wanted her to be happy. Ralph still believes she has a chance at happiness; she is young and can change her life for the better. He urges her to stay on at Gardencourt and to consider her next move. Isabel is terribly distraught as she watches Ralph dying before her eyes.

The next morning when Isabel awakens, she is certain she has seen the ghost of Gardencourt in the form of Ralph. Perhaps she has suffered enough, at last, to be able to see the phantom. Then she goes to her cousin's room and learns that he has died. In his will, Ralph leaves most of his fortune to charity; Gardencourt is inherited by his mother. Ralph leaves nothing to Isabel.

A few days after the funeral, Lord Warburton comes to visit and is surprised to find Isabel still there. He speaks to her in the garden, blushing and stammering a bit, and asks her to visit him and his sisters at Lockleigh before she returns to Italy. Isabel realizes that Warburton is still in love with her, but she tells him she doesn't have time to visit his estate this trip. She promises to visit him on another occasion.

As night falls, Caspar Goodwood, who had traveled with Ralph to England from Rome, finds Isabel alone in the garden. With great urgency, he insists that Isabel sit down and listen to him. He says he knows that Isabel is terribly unhappy in her marriage. Ralph told him everything when they were traveling together, and Ralph

made Caspar promise that he would look after Isabel. Now Caspar wants Isabel to stay with him and never return to Rome. He loves her more than ever and promises to take care of her for the rest of her life. Then he embraces Isabel and kisses her passionately. Isabel rushes back to the house, the darkness a blur around her.

Two days later, Caspar knocks on Henrietta's door in London. He expects to find Isabel waiting for him, but Henrietta tells him that Isabel stayed with her for only one night and then left to return to Italy. Caspar is jolted by the news and Henrietta tries to console him. "Just wait," she tells him, meaning that he is still young with plenty of time to fall in love with another woman. Caspar is crushed, however, feeling as if, in an instant, he has aged 30 years.

Analysis

When Isabel learns that Ralph is dying, she is, of course, terribly upset and can think only of seeing her cousin one more time before his death. Displaying an utter disregard for his wife's feelings, Osmond's attitude is heartless and cruel. He reveals his contempt for Isabel and her family, making no attempt to comfort his wife; Osmond, as usual, is concerned only with appearances: how will it look for his wife to travel alone to England? He scoffs at reports of Ralph's dying, saying, "He was dying when we married; he'll outlive us all." Osmond's callousness is exemplified by his refusal to embrace or comfort his wife. Ever the poseur, Osmond remains at his drawing table, engaged with his "art," copying a picture of an antique coin. When he finally stands, to acknowledge Isabel, he does so with a threat, hinting he will get back at her if she disobeys him to go to England. When Isabel accuses Osmond of disapproving of everything she does, Osmond turns pale and with a "cold smile" he says, "That's why you must go then? Not to see your cousin, but to take a revenge on me." When Isabel replies, "I know nothing about revenge," Osmond threatens her, declaring, "I do. Don't give me an occasion." He then accuses her of plotting a "calculated opposition," even though Isabel has just received the telegram from her aunt. Isabel and Osmond have completely exposed their feelings now, and when Isabel leaves for England, she is all too aware of the possible consequences of her action.

Countess Gemini's revelation is a stunning blow to Isabel. Following her hateful conversation with Osmond, Isabel finally learns the truth behind her marriage to him. She understands, at last, why Osmond feels such little regard for her, and why Madame Merle was so intent on having her marry him. She also realizes that her own actions and her refusal to listen to the advice of her friends and family have ultimately led her astray. She was deceived by others, and she fooled herself. Now she is condemned to a loveless marriage and has sacrificed other opportunities that might have given her a chance for happiness. Dorothea Krook, in her essay on the novel, asserts, however, that Osmond is also a victim. Like Isabel, he was manipulated by Madame Merle and during their courtship was even in love with the young woman. But Isabel was not the obedient lump of clay Osmond desired. Krook notes that Osmond "has been misled into a fatal error of judgment which has helped to precipitate the catastrophe...." Krook goes on to explain that, although Isabel desires to be a loyal wife, "it is impossible for her, being what she is, not to voice her idea—her moral idea—about many things in the life of her husband and the life of the society into which she has been drawn by her marriage." Osmond cannot bear it when Isabel's independent mind and criticisms are leveled at him.

At the convent, Isabel renews her commitment to Pansy. Pansy is afraid she will never see Isabel again; she knows that Isabel is her only ally, her only defense against Osmond. By promising to return to see her, Isabel refuses to sever all ties with Osmond; she has an opportunity to flee and never see him again, but she knows she cannot abandon Pansy. Isabel also meets with Madame Merle at the convent, but this relationship Isabel is determined to sever. Even when Madame Merle reveals the truth about Isabel's inheritance, Isabel refuses to respond or engage in a petty debate. She never wants to see the woman again and tells her so.

At Ralph's deathbed, Isabel is assured that her cousin only had her best interests at heart. He wanted her happiness, something he still wishes for and believes she can attain if she changes her present situation. After Ralph's death, Isabel is finally able to admit to Mrs. Touchett that she was right all along; she should never have married Gilbert Osmond. But when Lord Warburton calls on her, Isabel still cannot accept his stumbling advances. He is, perhaps, offering her one last chance to be with someone who respects her, but Isabel, while capable of opposing her husband, is still a slave to social propriety. She is a "lady" and will not enter into the scandal of divorce. Caspar, too, offers her a chance of escape, but again, Isabel rejects him in favor of returning to a loveless marriage.

Why does Isabel turn down a chance at freedom, only to return to a husband who loathes her? Oscar Cargill, writing in *The Novels of Henry James*, believes that Isabel "resists because all that she has learned about the folly of complete feminine liberty rushes in on her." According to Cargill, Isabel flees when she is confronted with the "prospect of an empty independence like her aunt's" and chooses to return to Italy to fulfill "her duty to her husband and her promise to Pansy, with all it entails"—a choice that seems to Isabel "to afford a more meaningful life." In reading *Henry James*, Louis Auchincloss, contends that, because Isabel is not afraid of Osmond, her primary concern is with "the ugliness of a public rupture of her marriage, of demonstrating her private failure to the world." He goes on to say that Isabel "has agreed to be (Osmond's) wife before the world, and this she will be while she has breath in her body. For better or worse. That was to be a lady in her time." Finally, according to Arnold Kettle, in his essay "Henry James: The Portrait of a Lady," it is ultimately a sense of duty that compels Isabel to return to her husband. Kettle notes that it is "inescapable that what Isabel finally chooses is something represented by a high cold word like duty or resignation, the duty of an empty vow, the resignation of the defeated, and that in making her choice she is paying a final sacrificial tribute to her own ruined conception of freedom."

Study Questions

1. Does Osmond consider himself to be an honorable man?

2. When did Osmond's first wife die and why do most people believe she was Pansy's mother?

3. When does Isabel finally decide to visit Ralph, against Osmond's wishes?

4. How does Pansy behave in the convent?

5. Who meets Isabel at the train station in London?

6. Why is Isabel surprised to learn that Henrietta will be moving to London?

7. How is Isabel greeted when she arrives at Gardencourt?

8. What message does Mrs. Touchett send to Sir Matthew Hope, the celebrated physician?

9. How does Caspar describe Isabel and Osmond?

10. As Ralph nears the end of his life, how does Henrietta feel about him?

Answers

1. In spite of his heartless attitudes and selfish actions, Osmond tells Isabel "What I value most in life is the honour of a thing!"

2. Because Osmond's wife died shortly after Madame Merle gave birth to Pansy, Osmond was able to lie and pretend his wife was Pansy's real mother.

3. Isabel decides to go to England after Countess Gemini tells her that Madame Merle is Pansy's mother.

4. Pansy is tearful and subdued, although she tries to remain cheerful. She wears a "little black dress" and is confined to the upstairs rooms of the convent.

5. Henrietta and Mr. Bantling meet her at the Charing Cross station.

6. Henrietta was always very critical of Europe in comparison to the United States. Now that Henrietta is getting married, Isabel is surprised that her friend plans to "give up" her country.

7. Because the new servants don't know who Isabel is, they greet her "coldly," showing her to a sitting room to wait for her aunt.

8. Because Ralph doesn't care for the man, he asks his mother to tell Sir Matthew that he died. However, Mrs. Touchett simply writes to the doctor telling him that her son dislikes him.

9. Caspar says, "You're the most unhappy of women, and your husband's the deadliest of fiends."

10. Henrietta has grown quite fond of Ralph, and after he dies, Henrietta inherits Ralph's library.

Suggested Essay Topics

1. Do you believe Madame Merle was solely responsible for ruining Isabel's life? Explain your answer.

2. Discuss Ralph's deathbed conversation with Isabel. Why does he believe Isabel still has a chance of finding happiness?

3. How is the title of the novel, *The Portrait of a Lady*, reflected in Isabel's decision to remain married to Osmond?

4. Compare the social attitudes of today with those of Isabel's time. How do you think Isabel might have acted if she was an independent young woman living in the 1990s?

Sample Analytical Paper Topics

Topic #1

Discuss the character of Isabel Archer in relation to Henry James's portrayal of the American in Europe.

Outline

I. Thesis Statement: The Portrait of a Lady *exemplifies James's depiction of the innocent American corrupted and damaged by European influences.*

II. Henry James: American and European

    A. James's exposure to and experience in Europe

    B. Raw American spirit versus refined European sensibility

III. Isabel Archer

    A. *The Portrait of a Lady*

        1. Isabel Archer as an innocent American

        2. Exposure to European culture, manners, and traditions

        3. Corrupting influences of Europe and Europeans

        4. American expatriates in Europe: Osmond and Madame Merle

5. Reactions of Isabel, Mrs. Touchett, and Henrietta to the Europeans

B. James's portrait of the "lady" abroad

1. Isabel's tragedy and loss of innocence

2. A loveless marriage: Isabel's fate in Europe

Topic #2

Discuss the role of women in European society. How does Isabel Archer's independent spirit reflect her Americanism?

Outline

I. Thesis Statement: *Isabel Archer must suppress her own independence and feminist spirit in order to become a European "lady."*

II. A portrait of an early feminist

A. Isabel Archer's independent spirit and intelligence

B. Differences with the "typical" European "lady" of the time

C. Independence and outspokenness as an alluring trait

1. Ralph Touchett's love of Isabel

2. Lord Warburton's "interesting" woman

3. Caspar Goodwood's American "lady"

D. Madame Merle as the Europeanized American woman

III. Marriage to Osmond

A. Isabel's attraction to Osmond

1. Intellectual qualities

2. Artistic qualities

B. Osmond's dislike of Isabel's "bad ideas"

1. Why ideas attract Ralph and Warburton

2. Why ideas repel Gilbert Osmond

C. Isabel's refusal to completely submit to Osmond

IV.   Isabel's fate

    A.   Surrender to societal conventions and return to Osmond

    B.   Sacrifice of self for Pansy

Topic #3

    Discuss James's use of "psychological realism" in *The Portrait of a Lady.*

Outline

I.   Thesis Statement: *In* The Portrait of a Lady, *James reveals much about his characters, not only through their actions, but also by directly revealing their innermost thoughts and feelings.*

II.   Isabel Archer's thoughts and emotions

    A.   On rejecting Lord Warburton's and Caspar Goodwood's proposals

        1.   Alone in the garden with Caspar's letter

        2.   With Warburton at lunch and in the gallery at Gardencourt

    B.   Feelings for Ralph and the Touchetts

    C.   Falling in love with Osmond and coldness of marriage

        1.   Walks in gardens with Osmond

        2.   Refusal to listen to the advice of others

        3.   Waiting for Caspar Goodwood after engagement to Osmond

        4.   Osmond as her husband and relation to Pansy

    D.   Pansy in the convent and return to Osmond

        1.   Isabel's devotion to Pansy

        2.   Caspar's kiss in the garden

III.   Osmond and Madame Merle

    A.   Introduction to Osmond

    B.   Madame Merle's relationship to Osmond

      1. Madame Merle's scheme

      2. Involvement of Isabel

  C. Osmond falls in love with Isabel

      1. Genuinely attracted to Isabel

      2. Discussion of Isabel's "bad ideas"

  D. Osmond's relationship with Madame Merle

  E. Isabel's admission of her "wretched" marriage to Gilbert Osmond

Bibliography

Anderson, Quentin. *The American Henry James.* New Brunswick, NJ: Rutgers University Press, 1957.

Auchincloss, Louis. *Henry James.* Minneapolis: University of Minnesota Press, 1975.

Bowden, Edwin T. *The Themes of Henry James.* New Haven: Yale University Press, 1956.

Buitenhis, Peter. *The Grasping Imagination.* Toronto: University of Toronto Press, 1970.

Cargill, Oscar. *The Novels of Henry James.* New York: Macmillan, 1961.

Edel, Leon. *Henry James.* Minneapolis: University of Minnesota Press, 1960.

James, Henry. *The Portrait of a Lady.* (An Authoritative Text with Reviews and Criticism, Edited by Robert D. Bamberg). New York: W. W. Norton & Company, 1975.

Kettle, Arnold. *An Introduction to the English Novel.* London: Hutchinson's University Library, 1953.

Krook, Dorothea. *The Ordeal of Consciousness in Henry James.* New York: Cambridge University Press, 1962.

Mazzella, Anthony J. "The New Isabel." In *The Portrait of a Lady* (An Authoritative Text with Reviews and Criticism, Edited by Robert D. Bamberg). New York: W. W. Norton & Company, 1975.